Learning to Teach:
A Critical Approach to Field Experiences

Second Edition

Learning to Teach:
A Critical Approach to Field Experiences

Second Edition

Natalie G. Adams
The University of Alabama

Christine Mary Shea
East Carolina University

Delores D. Liston
Georgia Southern University

Bryan Deever

LAWRENCE ERLBAUM ASSOCIATES, PUBLISHERS
2006   Mahwah, New Jersey   London

Lawrence Erlbaum Associates, Inc., Publishers
10 Industrial Avenue
Mahwah, New Jersey 07430
www.erlbaum.com

Cover design by Kathryn Houghtaling Lacey

Library of Congress Cataloging-in-Publication Data

Learning to teach : a critical approach to field experiences / Natalie G. Adams ... [et al.]. — 2nd ed.
      p. cm.
    Includes bibliographical references and index.
    ISBN 0-8058-5470-3 (pbk. : alk. paper)
1. Student teaching—United States. 2. Teachers—Training of—Social aspects—United States. 3. Observation (Educational method). 4. Criical pedagogy—United States.   I. Adams, Natalie G.
LB2157.U5L43   2005
370'.71'1—dc22   2005049473
                                                                              CIP

Books published by Lawrence Erlbaum Associates are printed on acid-free paper, and their bindings are chosen for strength and durability.

Printed in the United States of America
10 9 8 7 6 5 4 3 2

We dedicate the second edition of this book
to our friend and colleague, Bryan Deever (1955–2000).
Bryan was an ardent believer that teachers have the power
to change the world. His commitment to teacher education
and social justice continues to inspire us to light the spark
of social activism in our preservice teachers.

Contents

Section 3: Pedagogy and School Cultures: Issues of Race, Class, and Gender

Section 4: The School as an Ecosystem

Preface

When we began writing the first edition of this book in the 1990s, we were all teaching the Introductory Social Foundations of Education class at Georgia Southern University. At the time, the class required students to spend 3 weeks observing in a kindergarten through 12th grade public school classroom. From that class, students moved on to their block courses, which required limited participation in the classroom; then to their practicum course and an extended classroom participation experience; and finally to 10 weeks of student teaching. The first edition of this book emerged as a result of conversations and then collaborative efforts to design a 3-week observation experience that would assist preservice teachers in creating a critical and reflective dialogue with themselves, their assigned classroom cultures, and the larger school/community environment. Individually and collectively, we were committed to creating field experiences that not only initiated students into the culture of schools and teaching but also fostered a critical analysis of the intersections of race, class, gender, culture, power, politics, social transformation, and schooling. Our goal was to create a book that would allow us to translate our feminist, critical, and constructive postmodern perspectives into practice and to challenge traditional ways of thinking about the field experience, which are steeped in positivistic notions of research. Similar to most field experience textbooks, we wanted students to collect "hard evidence" about schools and classrooms, but more important, we wanted them to explore what this evidence says about the sometimes problematic nature, role, and dynamics of public schooling in the United States. In short, we wanted students to be more than passive observers of classroom techniques and strategies. As Britzman (1986) asserted, "Prospective teachers need to participate in developing critical ways of knowing with which they can interrogate school culture, the quality of students' and teachers' lives, and the particular role biography plays in understanding these dynamics" (p. 454).

Seven years have passed since the publication of the first edition of *Learning to Teach*. As in the first edition, the second edition of this text is still committed to taking as its starting point the lived experiences of preservice teachers, but those lived experiences must be viewed in the context of a very changed world since 1998. In the United States, we now live in a post-September 11th world in which xenophobia, violence, patriotism, citizenship, and democracy have taken on new meanings. Through the No Child Left Behind Act of 2001, the federal government is involved in public education in unprecedented ways, from determining what constitutes a "highly qualified" teacher to school districts having to prove they are not violating the Equal Access Act (1984) to high schools being required to give the names of senior students to military recruiters. Mandatory graduation exams, state writing tests, and annual standardized testing of student achievement are mainstays of most schools in the United States. Annual "report cards" of how our schools are educating all students are publicized on the front page of most local newspapers. Charter schools have proliferated in many states, and in 2002, the Supreme Court ruled in *Zelman v. Harris* (2002) that parents could use vouchers to send their children to parochial schools. Obesity has become a national health problem, while many states and school districts have eliminated physical education from their required course of study. Coke®, Dr. Pepper®, Taco Bell®, and McDonalds® are as much a part of today's schools as the U.S. Pledge of Allegiance. Because of these changes, what it means to go to school and teach in a school has changed dramatically. This edition includes activities that help preservice teachers explore the implications of these changes. We still believe this text is unique among field experience books. As one reviewer of the first edition stated, "few books offer something really new. But this one does." What this book continues to offer preservice teachers is a lens to see schools in a different light. Rather than telling the students what they should see as they observe in their schools, we ask them to consider how they might see differently.

Since writing the first edition of this book, our personal and professional lives have changed as well. Natalie and Delores have experienced schooling from a parent's perspective as we have watched our five children live, struggle, and, in some cases, thrive in public schools. Two of us have left Georgia Southern University. Christine is now a professor at Eastern Carolina University. Natalie went to Oklahoma State University and is now an associate professor at The University of Alabama. Delores, who is now a full professor at Georgia Southern University, made the transition from the quarter system to the semester system and was instrumental in revamping the teacher education program. Sadly, Bryan died in 2000. Until his death, he remained passionately committed to the belief that schools could be instruments of social transformation, and colleges of education must build teacher education programs around the theme of social justice. It is in memory of him that we write and dedicate this second edition of *Learning to Teach*.

HOW TO USE THIS BOOK

Given the diversity of field experience settings, formats, and duration, we wrote and organized this book with the intention that instructors and students would pick and choose those exercises most appropriate to their particular observation contexts and interests. Thus, the exercises are not meant to be completed sequentially. However, we do suggest that you complete some of the exercises in Section 1 prior to entering the field. These exercises are intended to provide a

stimulus for wider class discussions. We also recommend saving Section 6 until the field experience has been completed.

Each exercise follows a similar format: Background, Activity, Reflective Narrative, and Related Readings. The Background is a short introduction that provides context for the activities. The Activity section guides the observations. This is the "fact"-finding and data-gathering stage. The Reflective Narrative directs deeper thinking about the meaning and significance of what has been observed. The final section, Related Readings, gives a list of additional resources for further exploration of the topic.

ACKNOWLEDGMENTS

To Elizabeth Hendrix, Caren Penny, Marsha Zeagler, Serena Parris, Lee Digiovanni, Susan Ryan, Julie Rucker, Camille Shirah, and Scott Beck, we extend our deepest appreciation for all the help you gave us in making this second edition possible.

We continue to be thankful for Kate Cruickshank who thoughtfully left for us her teaching materials when she departed from Georgia Southern University. We also thank Dr. Jane Page and Dr. Fred Page from Georgia Southern for sharing the manuals they developed for foundations students and student teachers. It was Dr. Jane Page's manual "A Guide to Systematic Observation for Beginning Teacher Education Students," Kate's teaching materials, and the student teaching manuals created by Dr. Fred Page that provided the initial material and inspiration for this textbook.

We also thank Naomi Silverman, our editor, for her initial enthusiasm for this project and her continuing encouragement and support that enabled us to conceptualize, reconceptualize, and complete the first edition of the book and then, 7 years later, the second edition. She is truly a jewel. We thank the reviewers of the first edition and the revision survey respondents for the second edition, all of whom helped us to articulate more clearly the intentions and perspectives of this text. Finally, we express our thanks to all the undergraduate Foundations of Education students that we have taught over the past 10 years who have used and critiqued these exercises and whose valuable insights have made this a better and more meaningful text.

REFERENCES

Britzman, D. (1986). Cultural myths in the making of a teacher: Biography and social structure in teacher education. *Harvard Educational Review, 56,* 454.

Equal Access Act, 20 U.S.C. §§ 4071–74 (1984).

No Child Left Behind Act of 2001, Pub. L. No. 107–110, 115 Stat. 1425 (2002).

Zelman v. Harris, 536 U.S. 639 (2002).

Introduction

At the heart of this collection of classroom- and school-based activities, observations, and exercises is a reconceptualization of the notion of the field experience. Typically, a preservice teacher's first experience in the field is that of the "objective" observer who sits in a classroom to observe classroom practices "neutrally." Often, students are reminded to follow rules of objective research such as the following: The observer must observe the entire sequence or event; goals, limits, or guidelines must be set; the observation should be recorded completely and carefully; and observations must be as objective as possible. Embedded in this approach to the field experience is the assumption that if the student observer is immersed in what goes on in the field and given ample time to engage in a series of classroom observations, then he or she will emerge from the experiences with some form of truth about the real world of teachers, learners, the nature or knowledge and the subject matter, and classroom life.

Our text, however, aims to disrupt this conception of teacher education and field experiences. Rather, this text is intended to assist you, the preservice teacher, in taking a critical look at schools and the politics of schooling through the creation of a reflective dialogue among yourself, your assigned classroom, and the larger school environment. We emphasize the problematic nature and dynamics of public schooling and seek to encourage in you a greater awareness concerning your attitudes toward and connections with these educational processes.

Perhaps you are asking yourself, what does it mean to examine classrooms and schooling critically? We use the word *critical* in a very specific way. To be critical about schools means to bring to the forefront issues of power, politics, equity, and equality. It means raising questions about the relation between schools and the social and cultural reproduction of social classes, gender roles, and racial and ethnic prejudice. It means emphasizing the historical, social, political, and cultural factors responsible for shaping our present forms of schooling. It is important to remember that thinking critically about schools does not necessarily mean criticizing or being negative. By asking you to analyze critically the intersections of race, class, gender, power, knowledge, and schooling, we require that you be more than a passive observer of teaching techniques and strategies. Rather than telling you what you should see, we ask you to consider how you might see in a different way—a way that is admittedly grounded in a critical paradigm. Consequently, in some activities, we generate this context through both the background material and the questions posed in which certain points of view are supported and others are restricted or even eliminated. This is done because we believe very strongly that many issues, such as race and gender, are not solved problems of the past but are current issues that must be dealt with today.

By framing this book within a critical paradigm, we incorporate terms and concepts such as hegemony, ideology, and racial stratification that may not be familiar to you. These terms, along with the meanings they are given in this text, are important to understand before you continue this reading or enter the field. In the following section, we provide a brief overview of some of these terms and concepts in hopes that you might begin to develop a new language for describing what you see in the schools and classrooms you observe.

SOME IMPORTANT TERMS AND CONCEPTS

In part, this book is about the connections between culture, race, social class, and gender as well as the manner in which these intersect and intertwine within our pedagogy as teachers. Two concepts critical to such a sociocultural examination of schools and schooling are hegemony and ideology. *Hegemony*, a term with its origins in ancient Greece, at first described the manner in which one city-state exerted control over another through economic or political means rather than through direct military occupation. In a contemporary frame, this term refers to the manner in which individuals and social groups are controlled within a democratic society by some means other than the brute force of the military or police apparatus.[1] There are three players in this process that we now consider: social practices, social forms, and social structures. *Social practices* are outward forms of social expression found in words and language, gestures and rituals, and the various actions in which we daily engage within our social communities. One way of controlling individuals is to define what are acceptable and unacceptable social practices. In schools, a tremendous amount of time and energy is spent inducting young persons into those social practices considered appropriate in contemporary society. One might consider asking, however, whose definitions of "appropriate" drive this teaching, how these lessons become embedded in both the curriculum and the daily routines of school life, and why these social practices go relatively unchallenged.

Social practices are regulated through the social forms and social structures of a society. These are the formal arrangements of laws *(social forms)* and informal arrangements of common wisdom *(social structures)* that sanction certain social practices and not others. Schools are one of the principle sites where youth are taught what social practices represent "normal" life. Whereas social forms are visible and codified, social structures are those less discernible constructions that limit individual life. These appear to be naturally occurring divisions beyond the control of the individual. In the United States, for instance, people often speak of a "class structure," even though this country is purportedly egalitarian offering no one the rank

and title of royalty. It is assumed, however, that these social divisions do exist and that individuals reside somewhere on this socioeconomic landscape with little or no control over what defines the various class positions. This belief, however, limits the actions available to us. The same situation exists for other social structures such as those of race and gender. What does this have to do with education? Schools are one of the primary sites for teaching youth to believe in both the existence and the "inherent rightness" of social structures.

Social practices, forms, and structures serve to organize and sanction social actions. The knowledge, ideas, values, and beliefs produced and reproduced within these arrangements are what we refer to as *ideology*. Simply put, ideology is the assumed right way of seeing the world. As these ideas and practices become intertwined and embedded in our daily lives, individuals come to accept many things simply as common sense truth. As a social form, for example, the laws of most states restrict the social practice of marriage to heterosexual unions. Ideology supports those laws by generally defining *homosexuality* as "deviant."

In another example, the belief that Whites are genetically superior to other races was an ideological "truth" that guided social life for generations in this country. For example, at one time, it was commonly known "fact" that African Americans were intellectually inferior to Euro-Americans because of a difference in the average male skull size.[2] On the basis of this (and other) racist ideology, laws were enacted to limit and deny the constitutional rights of African American citizens of this country, and separate and unequal school systems were established and perpetuated to accommodate the "intellectual and psychological differences of the races."[3]

Another subtle manifestation of ideology is the way in which certain words become embedded in our public discourse while serving to limit and restrict (or even segregate) portions of the population. The word *ethnic* has come to be applied solely to persons of color. In this sense, ethnic issues are understood to be those issues of concern to particular minorities. However, we all have ethnic histories. The inaccurate belief that Euro-Americans are not ethnic serves to segregate one portion of the population from another and sets the European tradition up as the normal backdrop against which other ethnic perspectives are displayed.[4] Using the metaphor of computer software, ideology positions European ethnicity as the default setting. Everything else is different.

The same can be said of gender. In contemporary society, "gender issues" are those perceived to be of interest only to women and feminists. Gender studies programs at colleges and universities usually are understood as being reserved for women. Issues relating specifically to men are not regarded as gender issues. Of course, we are all gendered individuals, but ideology positions the masculine as the default setting—the marker of normality.

Ideological beliefs exist at multiple levels in our society—at both macrolevels and microlevels. A dominant ideology is the beliefs and values accepted and shared by the majority of individuals in a community/society (or at least that group holding power and privilege). An ideology of schooling, then, includes those beliefs and values accepted by education workers and students as the common sense approach to the daily practice of "doing school." Consider the following "facts": There is always a right answer, intelligence can be measured, and human development always occurs in discrete and regulated stages.[5]

What impact do these concepts have on the daily work of teachers? One primary effect of ideology is the manner in which it influences pedagogy. More than teaching methods or techniques, *pedagogy* is the integrated package of what teachers do as mediated through ideological beliefs. Some mistakenly equate pedagogy with method, but this is only one small portion of the whole. Pedagogy includes teaching strategies and techniques; beliefs, values, and personal assumptions about the world; and what we believe

to be the reasons and purposes of schooling. Pedagogy speaks to the entire constellation of who we are and what we do as teachers. All of this is informed, in turn, by our personal perspectives (influenced by ideology) and the sum of our identities. Driven by our cultural understandings of the world, these identities are constituted by the multiple intersections of race, social class, and gendered selves. These are all primary aspects of the culturally constructed self.

Another effect of ideology is on the content and construction of the school curriculum. Actually, there are several forms of curriculum operating simultaneously in any school at any given time. The overt or formal curriculum is the body of official knowledge that usually carries some kind of institutional endorsement, either from the state or the district. This formal curriculum is also an ideological document. The decisions about what is necessary to be officially educated (i.e., receive a diploma) are largely informed by ideology. Why is certain knowledge included and other knowledge excluded from the official curriculum? True, teachers cannot teach everything, but that still does not answer the question of why some knowledge is important and included, whereas other knowledge is less important and excluded.

This excluded knowledge is sometimes referred to as the *null curriculum*. This is the structured silence, constructed by schools, about certain issues and perspectives. The null curriculum is just as purposeful as the formal curriculum. Someone, or some group, must make a conscious decision about what to exclude from the formal curriculum: hence, in the null curriculum. These decisions are all based on ideological and cultural beliefs about what is and is not important knowledge.

Culture is the multitude of ways in which groups and individuals both live out and make sense of the conditions as well as the social and material environs of their lives.[6] Culture is not some set of artifacts, although there are forms of cultural production such as painting, music, and dance. Rather, culture is the social practices and ideological constructions individuals use to make sense out of and give order to their worlds. People do not inhabit cultures but live out cultural relations. We do not put on culture as one would don an article of clothing, although clothing might be a form of cultural expression. Rather, culture is produced in the interchange between self and the world. Within this transactional dialogue, social actions are driven by culture, although those same actions simultaneously define and redefine culture in the spheres in which we circulate. Thus, culture is continually in a dynamic state of reiteration and redefinition.[7]

Culture is something that is produced in our society. In this book, we examine the roles of public schools in the production and reproduction of culture. As schools interconnect with both local communities and the larger social whole, they form complex systems within which individuals circulate. As individuals move within these venues, they produce cultural understandings, artifacts, and meanings. Thus, culture is produced by people trying to make sense of the limitations constructed by social forms and structures in contemporary society.

Public schools are one place where individuals with different cultural perspectives come together on a regular basis. At once, schools become sites of cultural interaction and contestation. However, schools do not exist as some neutral playing field on which these relations are played out. Schools themselves are culturally constructed sites that perform a filtering function. By designating certain cultural beliefs and actions as acceptable and others as deviant, the schools value and devalue specific cultural perspectives. The complexity begins to arise, however, when we recognize that individuals are sophisticated intersections of multiple cultural perspectives.

People do not circulate individually in a single cultural sphere. This is far too simplistic and offers a view of culture based on some gross generalizations that may lead to severe stereotyping. For instance, what is Black culture or White culture? Do all African Americans or Euro-Americans share the same cultural base and see the world in exactly the same way? Of course they do not and neither do any of the other large social groups identified in contemporary society. As social beings, people are the intersection of multiple cultural points found in their ethnicity, social class, sex, gendered identities, sexual orientation, religion, geographical region, and the like. Further, these constructions are hermeneutic and change over time as individuals move in and out of various social settings, accumulate new experiences, and meet new people. All people live out multiple cultural relations simultaneously in sophisticated sets of dynamic constructions. This is fundamentally different from viewing culture as artifacts on a museum wall.

Yet why are those museum artifacts somehow perceived as forms of high cultural expression and representative of serious culture? How is serious culture perceived as different from popular culture? This dichotomy of serious and popular evokes some sense of the elite versus the masses, and this is one way that cultural questions help to understand how power is produced and manifested in the wider social order. In every place, there are dominant social groups who control the material and symbolic wealth of a community/society. Those groups construct cultural practices and representations that affirm their central values, interests, and concerns. These practices and representations affirm the dominant culture.

Some assert that the central purpose of formal education is to induct youth into the culture of a community/society.[8] The question then centers on whose cultural practices and representations are reproduced in the content, organization, structures, and rituals of schools. Most likely, it is the cultural practices and ideological truths of the dominant group. These are the groups who many times control schools at multiple levels: school board members, faculty, administrators, state education officials, textbook writers, professors of education, and so forth. This should not be seen as some sinister plot but rather as the result of particular social groups controlling the content and conduct of public schooling. Typically, people believe their cultural perspectives to be the best (the result of ideology). Therefore, if one is in a position to control the content of schools, one will probably want one's own perspective to be taught to the youth of a community.

We might ask, however, if it might not be dangerous to the elite to teach the dominant culture to the masses—to throw open a door of access for all. This is the point at which the multiplicity of culture plays an important role. Members of the elite are not simply those who manifest one set of cultural practices. They also must circulate within other "correct" cultural spheres such as those of social class, race, and gender. Schools, therefore, do not teach everyone how to circulate within those dominant social groups. Rather, the intention is to teach an appreciation of and a belief in the superiority of those forms of cultural expression found in the dominant culture and, by default, the natural superiority of those dominant social groups. For example, it is not necessary for working-class students to actually understand the complexities of Mozart or even appreciate the music. It is required only that they acknowledge this form of cultural expression as surpassing others such as rock, rap, country, jazz, and the like.

Where there are dominant social groups, there are also subordinate social groups and of course, subordinate cultures, sometimes referred to as minority cultures. However, to assume that there is one culture for each minority group in this country is again highly simplistic. One mistake made by many is assuming that minority and subordinate indicate some inherent inferiority. This is not the case at all. These individuals and groups simply do not have the same access to the material and symbolic wealth and resources of a community/society as do members of the dominant groups. Thus, *minority* and *subordinate* are quantitative terms indicating access, not qualitative terms indicating worth.

Another cultural cluster is subcultures: highly specialized subsets of either dominant or subor-

dinate groups. "Individuals who form subcultures often choose to display distinct symbols and engage in social practices that are offensive to the parent culture; they clearly establish an outside, oppositional identity."[9] Sometimes various subcultures move into mainstream prominence. In the 1960s, groups such as hippies, Black Panthers, and the American Indian Movement, to name a few, emerged to challenge the dominant culture of mainstream America. Within schools, small cadres of students exist who have carved out for themselves a subculture niche. You might be intimately familiar with such groups from your own life as a student.

All cultural groups express themselves through particular forms of music, dress, food, religion, dance, and language. These practices are more or less unique and have developed from the efforts of groups to shape their lives from their surrounding material and political environment. However, it is not unusual for one group (often the dominant social group) to appropriate and introduce to the mainstream cultural forms whose origins are in subordinate cultures or subcultures. One effect of this appropriation might be to redefine the original intentions of that particular cultural form. For example, rap music, appropriated from its origins in urban street culture by more mainstream artists such as Kid Rock, has been embedded within other musical forms and styles by artists such as Brittney Spears, Toby Keith, and Justin Timberlake. Whereas one effect is a more widespread hearing for rap artists, another is the homogenization of the form accomplished by severing the style from the cultural venue out of which it grew. Thus, mainstream rap is different fundamentally from original street versions and no longer functions as an effective cultural form for that segment of our urban population.

Along with the production of culture is the concurrent deconstruction of culture. *Deculturization* is the process of stripping away a person's culture and replacing it with other cultural forms, usually those of the dominant group.[10] The "civilizing" of the children of Native peoples and the "Americanization" of some immigrants to this country in the late 19th and early 20th centuries took deculturization as a primary objective. In this process, those who complied were deemed "educated," whereas those who resisted were considered ignorant. Deculturization was then understood as a desirable process because the cultural perspectives of other groups were judged inferior or even dangerous to the established social order. In nearly every instance, it is the dominant culture that engages in these forms of "cultural cleansing" with subordinate or minority cultures as the target of their efforts.

In contemporary society, some groups have more influence than others in the production of culture, sense, and meaning, not because their positions are superior but because they have greater access to the avenues of public communication such as the media, advertising, and the schools. Through the process of hegemony, the ideological messages of the dominant culture are infused throughout our daily lives. The growing corporate connections and expanding technological capabilities in contemporary society offer even wider avenues for the dissemination of particular cultural perspectives. Consider, for example, what some have termed the "Disney-fication" of our culture as the Disney Corporation infiltrates our daily lives through the purchasing of commercial television networks, publishing houses, and public lands.[11]

Now we turn our attention to three locations of cultural production investigated in this book. The first we will consider is *race*, an artificial social category for the grouping of humans based on the primary physical distinction of skin color that has no basis in scientific fact.[12] This grouping is usually used as a pretext for the inequitable distribution of material and symbolic wealth, resources, justice, or freedom. The smallest natural division of living creatures is species; therefore, any subdivision beyond that is a human construction. Many people, however, confuse race with ethnicity. Race is a socially constructed division based on physical distinctions, whereas ethnicity is a group of individuals

with a shared sense of peoplehood. Individuals with the same skin color do not necessarily share this sense of ethnic community.

A belief in race is nearly always accompanied by a set of normative stereotypes assigned to a particular group on the basis of their skin color. Think about the larger stereotypes in our society: Asian Americans are inherently excellent in mathematics, African Americans in sports, Euro-Americans in advanced academics, and so on. Although these stereotypes are based on popular mythology, they have become embedded in our ideologies. A direct parallel would be to argue that all brunettes are inherently excellent in mathematics, red heads in sports, and blondes in advanced academics. This may sound silly, but these assumptions are based on exactly the same defining criteria: physical appearance.

Belief in racial characteristics fosters discriminatory practices. *Racial stratification* is the construction of human strata (in the geological sense) on the basis of skin color, which justifies unequal distribution of and the inequitable access to material and symbolic wealth. In other words, the closer your group is to the top, the more you get. *Racism* is the ideology that justifies racial stratification, and *racist acts* are those actions based on racism through which racial stratification is reinforced and perpetuated. Thus, racist acts occur because people hold racist beliefs and act on those beliefs. Those actions result in the perpetuation of racial stratification and division.

Institutional racism is the codification and bureaucratization of practices, knowledge, and values that both produce and justify the inequitable treatment of people on the basis of race. Institutional racism can occur in any social organization, even if the individuals in the institution are not themselves perpetuating racist acts. For instance, you might work in a school that tracks students through the use of tests that are prejudicial toward certain groups. This does not necessarily make you a racist, but the construction of the institutional practices around you might be racist.

The primary point is this: Although the basic assumption of race is an illusion (albeit convenient for some), the effects generated by and the actions committed in the name of race are very real and concrete parts of our daily lives. The question, then, is what roles do schools play in this process? If we teach only about getting along with one another and tolerating other races (i.e., Black History month), we fail to address the basic issue that race is an illusion in the first place. In the name of prejudice reduction, we are treating the symptoms and not the disease. Prejudice, however, should not be confused with racism, although racial prejudice does exist. *Prejudice* is the irrational suspicion or hatred of an individual or group formed without an examination of that individual or group. This is not to say that exposure will guarantee a reduction in prejudicial attitudes. How many times have we heard someone refer to a person from another cultural group as "a credit to their ..."? Everyone is prejudiced at one time or another in their social lives. The key is to resist acting on those prejudices and to attempt overcoming our irrational fears of "the other."

The second source of cultural production is *social class*, defined through the economic and political relationships found within a given society. Class cultures are produced by individuals and groups living under constraints of income level, occupation, place of residence, and other indicators of status and social rank. Again, people do not inhabit social classes but live out class relations, some of which might be simultaneously dominant and subordinate. As with any cultural phenomenon, social class is generative and produces particular forms of culture that serve to define and maintain class boundaries.

Finally, there is gender. Like race, gender is another socially constructed term. In the discourse of public life, many people wrongly use "sex" and "gender" interchangeably. *Sex* is the biological distinction of male or female and is grounded in one's role in the reproductive process. *Gender* is a set of social definitions (mas-

culine and feminine) that are fluid and change over time. Much of the confusion occurs when individuals mistakenly attribute stereotypical gender characteristics with sexual roles: Females are genetically nurturing and dependent, whereas males are genetically strong and independent. Again, this artificially constructed concept leads to concrete effects in the forms of sexism, sexual stratification, sexist acts, and institutional sexism (i.e., "the glass ceiling").

A NOTE ON OBSERVING IN CLASSROOMS

One purpose of this text is to provide you with a guide to help structure observations and field experiences in schools. In some ways, the familiarity with classrooms hinders observation. Because each of us has spent quite a lot of time in classrooms already, our tendency is to continue the activities familiar to us. That is, we have been students in classrooms for at least a dozen years. We are accustomed to sitting quietly at our desks, paying attention to the teacher, noticing things other students are doing (e.g., talking, passing notes, taking notes, etc.) but trying not to let these activities distract us from learning the subject matter. Thus, our tendency is to focus our attention on the content the instructor is teaching. As students, the content was our most important focus, and noticing other things was a distraction.

During the field experience/observation, the major focus of attention needs to shift. No longer is content the main focus. Here, the content or subject matter may become a distraction. When the teacher writes something on the board, this is not a signal to put this in your notebook. Instead, during this type of observation, you may find a variety of aspects important. For example, you may note the type of material the teacher puts on the board. Is it a summary of main points, key words or vocabulary, or is it a student's name singled out for praise or reprimand? In contrast, your observation might focus more on how students respond to the teacher as he or she writes on the board. For example, do they duplicate the information on the board in their notes, or do they take the opportunity to engage in other activities? Your observation may need to account for both of these aspects.

The exercises in this book provide you with a guide to help focus your attention away from the content or course material of a classroom and toward what is happening in the classroom and why. Why is the classroom organized as it is? Why is the teacher standing in a particular location? Why does the teacher move around at some times and not at others? Assuming that schools reflect society, how is society reflected by the school/classroom you are observing? Some of these questions might produce tension as you watch the teacher doing things with which you might not agree. This is healthy. This tension is an indicator that you are aware of the multiple layers of meaning and interaction occurring in the classroom. Such awareness can only be an asset in your later work.

Some of the exercises focus on schools in broad terms and address larger questions; others focus on specific interactions in particular classroom situations. Our goal is to provide a framework for activity that helps you address these and other questions. Finally, because schools are not neat little compartments of interaction, there is some overlap between certain exercises (e.g., dress codes and regulating the body). This overlap is not a weakness or repetition because we are asking you to look at the same phenomenon from more than one perspective.

You will notice that the text is organized around the following six themes:

1. Preobservational activities: The exploration of self.
2. Regulation of the "schooled" body.
3. Pedagogy and school cultures: Issues of race, class, and gender.
4. The school as an ecosystem.
5. No child left untested.
6. After the field experience: Now what?

In Section 1, we take as its starting point the everyday lived experiences of preservice teachers. In Section 2, we focus on questioning how policies and practices of schools may operate to control what constitutes appropriate raced, gendered, classed, and sexualized student and teacher bodies. In Section 3, we examine the critical aspects of classrooms structures, teaching, and learning. In Section 4, we illuminate some of the competing metaphors that underlie the organizational culture of public schools. In Section 5, new to this second edition, we question the implications of No Child Left Behind Act of 2001,[13] standards, and accountability on the everyday doing of school. In Section 6, we challenge students to redesign aspects of schools, schooling, and teacher education.

It is our hope that this book encourages you to engage in critical observations of and reflections on your field experiences including the production of personal narratives and an understanding that the work of education exists at multiple (and sometimes contradictory) levels of meaning.

NOTES

[1]McLaren, P. (1989). *Life in schools*. New York: Longman.

[2]Gould, S. J. (1981). *The mismeasure of man*. New York: Norton.

[3]*Plessey v. Ferguson*, 163 U.S. 256 (1896).

[4]Roman, L. G. (1993). White is a color/White defensiveness, postmodernism, and anti-racist pedagogy. In C. McCarthy & W. Crichelow (Eds.), *Race, identity, and representation in education* (pp. 71–88). New York: Routledge.

[5]See Cornbleth, C. (1987). The persistence of myth in teacher education and teaching. In T. S. Popkewitz (Ed.), *Critical studies in teacher education: Its folklore, theory and practice* (pp. 186–210). New York: Falmer.

[6]McLaren, *op.cit.*, p. 171.

[7]O'Connor, T. (1989). Cultural voice and strategies for multicultural education. *Journal of Education, 17*, 57–74.

[8]Schubert, W. H. (1986). *Curriculum: Perspectives, paradigms, and possibility*. New York: Macmillan.

[9]McLaren, *op.cit.*

[10]Spring, J. (1994). *Deculturalization and the struggle for equality: A brief history of the education of dominated cultures in the United States.* New York: McGraw-Hill.

[11]Giroux, H. A. (1996). *Fugitive cultures: Race, violence, and youth* (pp. 89–113). New York: Routledge.

[12]deMarrais, K., & LeCompte, M. (1995). *How schools work: A sociological analysis of schooling* (2nd ed., p. 222). New York: Longman.

[13]No Child Left Behind Act of 2001, Pub. L. No. 107–110, 115 Stat. 1425 (2002).

Section 1

Preobservational Activities: The Exploration of Self

INTRODUCTION

Education has a unique position among the professional fields. Students majoring in education do not begin to study their field with a blank slate. Instead, preservice teachers enter their programs with a plethora of preconceived notions about what it means to be a teacher. Unlike the fields of architecture or electrical engineering in which students often do not come into contact with architects or engineers before choosing their major, each of us has had rich and personal experiences with a variety of teachers. Before deciding to become a teacher, each of us spent a lot of time in classrooms as students. All education majors (indeed all majors) have had the opportunity to learn a lot about the profession of teaching. We all know much of what teachers do and have witnessed several teachers practicing their art. This knowledge colors the way we perceive the profession of education as we embark on a career in the field.

Knowing so much about the schooling process can be both an advantage and a disadvantage for preservice teachers. The advantages are obvious in that education majors begin with some knowledge of their chosen profession. The disadvantages emerge as education majors discover, once the perspective of a teacher is gained, that some of their ideas about education, which developed from the vantage point of a student, are erroneous. For example, few students perceive the amount of paperwork required of the average school teacher or the hours it takes a teacher to grade papers and prepare for the next day's lessons.

Your teacher education program has been designed to help you make the transformation from student to teacher. One of the first steps in this transformation involves self-reflection and understanding. To transmit knowledge and cultural traditions (values), we must first explore ourselves to know which knowledge and values ought to be perpetuated. Thus, teachers must be reflective practitioners, and the first step in becoming a reflective practitioner is to know yourself. The family roles we take on, the personal cultures we adopt, the religious beliefs to which we adhere, the traditions and observances we celebrate, all are a part of who we are.[1] As teachers, we reflect these values through our presence in the classroom and pass these values on to our students.

A second aspect of becoming a reflective practitioner calls for the interrogation of one's "institutional biography."[2] As students, we have participated in school rituals and routines; we have passed and failed courses. We have obeyed and disobeyed rules. We have been insiders and outsiders of groups, organizations, teams, and cliques. These collective school experiences constitute our biography. Part of the transformation from student to teacher takes place as our biography shifts in focus from the role of student to the role of teacher.[3] In moving to the front of the classroom, beginning teachers should reflectively critique their own school experiences and resulting beliefs about education.

For this reason, we begin this book with a series of activities designed to encourage you to look closely at yourself and the beliefs you have about schools based on your prior experiences.

The intention of these exercises is to encourage you in becoming more reflective about who you are and then about how aspects of your identity contribute to and are influenced by the culture of school.

The exercise in Called To Teach is intended for use early in your observation period. Here, you will have an opportunity to think and write about why you want to become a teacher. This exercise will help you discover if your expectations of the profession of teaching match the experiences of others.

The exercise in Significant Past School Experiences invites you to remember some of your own kindergarten through 12th grade experiences. Because many important events happen to us as we progress through school, we as teachers have a great responsibility to be aware of their power over the lives of children. In completing this exercise, you will be encouraged to remember some of your own positive and negative formative school experiences so that you can be mindful of the power teachers and peers exhibit over students. As you become a teacher, keep in mind that you will play a similar role in the lives of your students.

Finding a Sense of Place is an exercise that is intended to help you learn more about yourself through discovering your own comfort places. Knowing more about what spaces make you comfortable will enable you to create more comfortable spaces for yourself and for your future students.

The exercises in Multicultural Self, Prevailing Privileges, and Cultural Portrait focus on the topic of identity. These exercises encourage you to look at why you are the way you are. How have your gender, race, ethnicity, social class, and physical abilities contributed to your sense of self and your construction of others? These aspects of our identity affect the ways in which we have been treated in school and thus impact our educational and career choices. They also impact how we view others. These exercises will provide you with new ways of understanding yourself in the culture of school.

Related Readings

Delpit, L. (1995). *Other people's children: Cultural conflict in the classroom.* New York: New Press.

Gatto, J. T. (2003). *The underground history of American education.* New York: Oxford Village Press.

Goodlad, J. I. (1984). *A place called school.* New York: McGraw-Hill. (Original work published 1984)

Gordon, J. A. (2002). The color of teaching. *Journal of Teacher Education, 53*(2), 123–127.

Ladson-Billings, G. (1994). *The dreamkeepers: Successful teachers of African American children.* San Francisco: Jossey-Bass.

Martin, J. R. (1992). *The schoolhome: Rethinking schools for changing families.* Cambridge, MA: Harvard University Press.

Noddings, N. (1992). *The challenge to care in schools.* New York: Teachers College Press.

Sidorkin, A. M. (2002). *Learning relations: Impure education, deschooled schools & dialogue with evil.* New York: Peter Lang.

CALLED TO TEACH

Background

Do you believe that you have been called to teach? Teaching is a rewarding and exciting career choice. Opportunities abound to positively impact the lives of children. Teachers stimulate the intellectual growth of children, participate in the perpetuation of our culture and heritage, and "touch lives" in significant ways.

Each year, approximately 200,000 new teachers enter the profession[4]. However, approximately one third of beginning teachers leave the field of teaching within the first 3 years.[5] What causes this relatively high attrition rate? What happens to the energy and enthusiasm of these newly minted teachers? As a prospective teacher, these questions are probably important to you.

Two factors that can enhance the potential of new teachers to remain in education are increased mentoring[6] and a greater awareness of what the field of teaching entails.[7] Over the past few years, more schools and school districts have worked hard to implement teacher mentoring programs. Schools are doing their part to address this concern and prepare to support your career choice.

Preservice teachers, like you, also need to work hard to make sure that teaching is the right career choice. One way that you can be better prepared to take full advantage of teacher mentoring programs is to be well-informed about your chosen profession. This exercise is designed to provide you with an opportunity to reflect on your reasons for becoming a teacher.

Activity

What are your reasons for becoming a teacher? Some people enter teaching because they "love children" or expect to have summers off. Others want to teach because they perceive teaching as a career in which one can easily balance work and family. Still others feel family or social pressure to teach. Start by making a list of all the reasons you want to major in education and begin a career in teaching.

After you have a list, investigate these reasons more deeply. Are your reasons for entering the profession of teaching realistic? Are they reasonable outcomes to expect in the field of teaching? Conduct an investigation to find out.

If you have friends or relatives who are teachers, talk with them and listen to what they have to say about your reasons for teaching. Ask them about their reasons for teaching. Compare their experiences with your expectations. Do they match? Why or why not?

Conduct an Internet search for key words and phrases among your reasons for teaching. Are your reasons for wanting to become a teacher shared by current teachers? Do your expectations of the job of teaching seem appropriate and reasonable?

Does the career ladder of teaching match your expectations? What do teachers do to earn raises? Are these the kinds of activities that you are interested in doing? Again, do your expectations of the job match the requirements of the field?

Reflective Narrative

One common motivation to enter the field of teaching that we hear from preservice teachers is "because I love children." A quick Internet search using the key words *teaching* and *I love children* came up with some interesting Web pages. One stated, "While I liked all the kids in the class, I hated the act of actually teaching them."[8] Teachers often experience burnout and isolation from other adults.[9] Before entering the teaching profession, consider what you will do to counteract feelings of isolation and retain your love of children.

What did you learn from this exercise? Are you sure teaching is the right career choice for you? Why or why not?

Related Readings

Ben-Peretz, M., & Schonmann, S. (2000). *Behind closed doors: Teachers and the role of the teachers' lounge.* Albany: State University of New York Press.

Cain, M. (2001). Ten qualities of the renewed teacher. *Phi Delta Kappan, 82,* 702–709.

Cornbleth, C. (1987). The persistence of myth in teacher education and teaching. In T. S. Popkewitz (Ed.), *Critical studies in teacher education: Its folklore, theory and practice* (pp. 186–210). New York: Falmer.

David, T. (2000). Teacher mentoring: Benefits all around. *Kappa Delta Pi Record, 36,* 134–136.

Greene, M. (1988). *Dialectic of freedom.* New York: Teachers College Press.

McLaren, P. (1989). *Life in schools: An introduction to critical pedagogy in the foundations of education.* New York: Longman.

McNergney, R. F., & Herbert, J. M. (1995). *Foundations of education: The challenge of professional practice.* Boston: Allyn & Bacon.

Parashar, A. (2005). Teaching kids—UGH!! (… and what I learned from it). Retrieved December 13, 2004, from http://www.howtoadvice.com/TeachingKids

Scherer, M. (Ed.). (2003). *Keeping good teachers.* Alexandria, VA: Association for Supervision and Curriculum Development.

SIGNIFICANT PAST SCHOOL EXPERIENCES

Background

From the perspective of a teacher, the daily events of a typical school day are just that—typical. Putting grades on papers, marking students present or absent, reprimanding the same students over and over for disruptive behavior, and struggling to create at least a handful of "teachable moments" during the course of a day all begin to take on a rather monotonous and routine flavor. Often, these events become routine for students as well. However, once in a while, something different happens, and the life of a student is changed forever.

The power of teachers and this vulnerability of students in classrooms is often overlooked. Receiving a smiley face or a gold star on a paper may seem like a trivial, quaint, or trite happening from the perspective of an adult, but in the eyes of a child who sees himself or herself being judged as acceptable or unacceptable, the event can loom very large. Other examples of formative experiences might include being the only Black student in the gifted program or being labeled as learning disabled.

These school experiences, both good and bad, have been formative. They have often occurred without the awareness of the teacher. Nevertheless, the teacher usually played a significant role in shaping such experiences, which need not have been part of the teacher's formal lesson plan. These events might not have been a direct part of the subject matter being taught at the moment. They occurred as side effects of a particular teaching style or as part of the human interaction between students or between students and teachers.

For teachers and future teachers, these events become teaching models to emulate or avoid. Critical teacher educators have argued that if preservice teachers do not interrogate and problematize their own past schooling experiences, then as new teachers, they will reproduce and perpetuate existing school practices that reflect the inequalities and prejudices in society.[10] For these reasons, this exercise encourages you to recall at least one significant experience for critical examination.

Activity

Spend some time reflecting on formative experiences you had in school (e.g., being chosen as lead star in the school play or being called on in math class and not knowing the answer). Start by making a list of these experiences. Then, select one or two to explore in depth. Try to remember details of the event. How old were you? What was the subject matter being taught? Who else was in the room or on the playground? What happened and why? Why was this event important to you? What has followed from the event? As a result of this experience, how have you behaved differently? What was it that made this experience stand out from the routine of your school experiences? Write a brief narrative about these experience(s).

Reflective Narrative

After remembering and reconstructing these events, reflect again on these experiences from the perspective of a teacher. Was this a type of experience you would want a student in your classroom to have? If so, what can you do to make this happen? If not, what can you do to keep your students from having this experience?

Having considered this event from your perspective as a student and from your perspective as a student and as a teacher, reflect again about its broader interpretations. Generalize from your particular experience. How does the event inform you about the roles, conditions, and interpretations of schools? Is this experience limited only to schools? Might it occur in a church, a shopping mall, a sporting event, alone in nature, and so on? Where does this event fit in the culture of school? Could any student share this experience, or is it unique to you personally or to those sharing your age, social class, race, and gender? What aspects of your identity went into the composition of this experience? How did the race, gender, age, and social class of the teacher serve to generate your interpretation of the experience? How did your expectations of school work to bring about this experience? How are these events related to achievement, competition, self-esteem, dignity, and the human spirit?

Related Readings

Britzman, D. (1986). Cultural myths in the making of a teacher: Biography and social structure in teacher education. *Harvard Educational Review, 56,* 442–456.

Greene, M. (1986). Perspectives and imperatives: Reflection and passion in teaching. *Journal of Curriculum and Supervision, 2,* 68–81.

Fordham, S. (1988). Racelessness as a factor in Black student's school success: Pragmatic strategy or pyrrhic victory. *Harvard Educational Review, 59,* 54–84.

Martin, J. R. (1985). Becoming educated: A journey of alienation or integration? *Journal of Education, 167*(3), 71–84.

Tatum, B. (1997) *Why are all the Black kids sitting together in the cafeteria? And other conversations about race.* New York: Basic Books.

FINDING A SENSE OF PLACE

Background

Self-discovery is among the most important processes in which you, as a future teacher, can be involved. As teachers, you will be guiding young children and adolescents on the path toward wholeness as human beings and toward living meaningful lives. For this reason, you must develop a strong sense of meaning for your own life.

The following activity is designed to provide you with an opportunity to define the conditions that make you feel most comfortable.[11] Here, you will define the characteristics of environments that are important for establishing and maintaining a "sense of place" for you.

Activity

Find your favorite spot at home or on campus. Go there, sit quietly, and think of other places where you have been happy and at ease. Are they places where you have lived or visited? Are they related to happy memories from childhood? Perhaps they are not in the home or at school. Are these places inside, or are they outdoors?

Next, consider why it is you chose this place? What aspects of this spot please you and why? In your mind, move around your favorite place. Take note of the smells, colors, textures, and ambiance. These various aspects inform you of the qualities you appreciate and the kinds of spaces that make you comfortable in your world.

Reflective Narrative

Where were you sitting while on this imaginary tour? Why did you choose this spot? We all have our own special places where we feel most at peace with ourselves and the world. Wherever it is—at the kitchen table, by a window, in the loft, or a garden hideaway—you should become aware of the unique features of your chosen space. Recognizing them will give you more insight into how you respond to the school and classroom environment in which you will be observing.

Related Readings

Aberley, D. (1993). *Boundaries of home: Mapping for local empowerment*. Philadelphia, PA: New Society Publishers.

Chawla, L. (1994). *In the first country of places: Nature, poetry, and childhood memory*. Albany: State University of New York Press.

Day, C. (1990). *Places of the soul: Architecture and environmental design as healing art*. London: Aquarian Press.

Gruenewald, D. A. (2003). Foundations of place: A multidisciplinary framework for place-conscious education. *American Educational Research Journal, 40,* 619–654.

Hiss, T. (1990). *The experience of place*. New York: Vintage Books.

LaChappelle, D. (1988). *Sacred land, sacred sex, rapture of the deep: Concerning deep ecology and celebrating life*. Durango, CO: Kaviki Press.

Nabhan, G. P., & Trimble, S. (1994). *The geography of childhood: Why children need wild places*. Boston: Beacon Press.

Sinclaire, C. (1994). *Looking for home: A phenomenological study of home in the classroom*. Albany: State University of New York Press.

MULTICULTURAL SELF

Background

Culture is a term that has received a great deal of press lately. Most individuals consider culture as the artifacts produced by a group of people. Although these artifacts are representations of culture, they are not culture itself. Others define culture as something you can acquire. In this sense, culture is understood as a commodity (like a loaf of bread) that one might somehow get through study or material acquisition (such as paintings, sculpture, season tickets to the opera, or a college course). As you acquire these things, you become more "cultured." Still others understand culture as being tied to race or ethnicity. These individuals often refer to African American, or Irish or Asian culture. According to a more contemporary reading, culture is the particular ways in which a social group lives out and makes sense of its given circumstances and conditions of life.[12]

One great confusion of culture is the belief that people are essentially monocultural, that we somehow reside in great monolithic blocks representing singular cultural perspectives based on some primary defining factor such as skin color. In this way, it might make sense to assume all Blacks see the world in one way, whereas all Whites see the world in another or that all women are naturally nurturing and caring, whereas all men are competitive and out of touch with their feelings. This simply is not true. In reality, we are intersections of multiple cultural positions that simultaneously might be contradictory and mutually supportive, coherent and incoherent. Our ethnicity, georegional origin, sex, religion, social class, sexual orientation, and dominant political orientation, to name a few factors, all intersect within us as individuals (e.g., an Irish, Catholic, working-class female). To make matters more confusing, these intersections shift and change through time as we gain new experiences and reflect on old experiences.

Activity

The purpose of this exercise is to explore and reflect on your own cultural intersections. Take some time to think about what and who you are as a multicultural being. It might be helpful for you to jot down a list or maybe produce some thematic web of cultural influences. After you have thoroughly investigated yourself, informally jot down how these different cultural positions color how you define your actions, your preferences, your prejudices, or realm of acceptable and unacceptable actions. How do these intersections work with each other? Are some contradictory, seeming to cancel one another? Are others mutually supportive? Where are these positions relative to the dominant culture within which you circulate? How might these positions influence your beliefs about teaching and the manner in which you might go about your work? After reflecting on these questions and jotting down your responses to them, write up a narrative to share with others.

Reflective Narrative

Are there some positions that you found in your life with which you are uncomfortable? How do you feel about those intersections that place you in minority positions or in dominant (i.e., majority or mainstream) positions? What changes might you make? What impact might these discoveries have on your approach to teaching or where you choose to teach? How might these discoveries color your way of looking at others, especially your students? Might it make a difference to understand individual students as complex social beings rather than within the monolithic block of students? How might the knowledge gained in this exercise aid your future work in education?

Related Readings

Banks, J. A. (2004). Multicultural education: Historical development, dimensions, and practice. In J. A. Banks & C. A. M. Banks (Eds.), *Handbook of research on multicultural education* (pp. 3–24). San Francisco: Jossey-Bass.

Carothers, S. (1990). Catching sense: Learning from our mothers to be Black and female. In F. Ginsberg & A. Tsing (Eds.), *Uncertain terms: Negotiating gender in American culture* (pp. 232–247). Boston: Beacon.

Fordham, S., & Ogbu, J. (1986). Black students' school success: Coping with the burden of "acting White." *The Urban Review, 18*, 176–206.

Irvine, J. J. (2003). *Educating teachers for a diverse society: Seeing with the cultural eye.* New York: Teachers College Press.

Ladson-Billings, G. (1994). *The dreamkeepers: Successful teachers of African American children.* San Francisco: Jossey-Bass.

McCarthy, C. (1990). *Race and curriculum: Social inequality and the theories and politics of difference in contemporary research and schooling.* London: Falmer.

PREVAILING PRIVILEGES

Background

Since the Civil Rights Movement of the 1960s, great strides have been made in our society to eliminate institutional prejudices. For example, we no longer see segregated drinking fountains and restrooms for Blacks and Whites, schools have been formally desegregated, women are beginning to obtain and even gain promotions within traditionally male-dominated fields, and the phrase "equal pay for equal work" is familiar and seems reasonable to almost all Americans.

In addition, our language reflects our commitments to eradicating prejudice. We are familiar with terms such as *racism*, *sexism*, and *sexual harassment*—the terms used to help recognize oppression. Furthermore, we are becoming familiar with terms that help overcome prejudice. Terms such as *multiculturalism* and *empowerment* are now also part of our everyday educational vocabulary.

Another step, however, in the fight for equality and the end of oppression is to interrogate our own personal sites of privilege. These privileges, or unearned rights, are of many kinds. For example, the prejudice that Japanese Americans are "naturally" better at math makes it more likely for some teachers to place a Japanese American student in an advanced calculus class than in a remedial math class without even looking at test scores or previously demonstrated academic ability. It is through this process of interrogation that we can begin to understand how we sometimes unknowingly perpetuate racism, oppression, and prejudice. Hopefully, through such

awareness, we can become better informed agents of change. Having recognized and begun the process of removing the oppressive and prejudicial conditions under which many Americans still struggle, we are ready to turn our attention to the advantages (privileges) some of us share.

Often these advantages are not one dimensional. Rather, they are based in and reveal the intersections of several preconceived and prejudicial notions (see Multicultural Self and Cultural Portrait exercises). Furthermore, these advantages are likely to be rooted in beliefs about gender and race or those of race and social class. Consider this example. The local basketball coach, assuming that African American males are better basketball players, may give them an advantage in tryouts for the team.

Activity

Make a list of at least 20 privileges you now enjoy. Include things you have taken for granted and assumed you deserve. For example, as a White woman, I know I can go into just about any supermarket and my check will be accepted, often without a show of identification.

Include also privileges you have been given that you probably did not deserve (e.g., the privilege to remain ignorant of the literary contributions of people of color). Such privileges are harmful for both the privileged and those denied privilege. Consider what you are missing by not knowing the work of writers such as Carlos Fuentes, Nikki Giovanni, Terry MacMillan,

Isabella Allende, Salman Rushdie, Amy Tan, and countless others who remain outside the mainstream literature curriculum of public schools. Consider also privileges of age. What advantages do you have now that you did not have before you came to college? What privileges do you perceive faculty members have that you do not? For example, often in college towns students (or people assumed to be students) have more difficulty renting a house or apartment than people assumed to be faculty members or local people.

Reflective Narrative

Now that you have made this list, look again at the contents. Some privileges are clearly unfair advantages that represent prejudicial treatment that should be eliminated. Others, however, are privileges now because they are available only to some people but ought to be extended to everyone.

Once you have made these distinctions, you are ready to take action. Go through the list one more time. This time, for each item on your list, write down one thing you can do to either help eliminate this privilege or extend it to others who are currently denied this advantage. Now, as the opportunity arises (or can be generated by you) put your ideas into action.

Related Readings

Deplit, L. (1988). The silenced dialogue: Power and pedagogy in educating other people's children. *Harvard Educational Review, 58,* 280–298.

Gay, G. (2000). *Culturally responsive teaching: Theory, research, and practice.* New York: Teachers College Press.

Howard, G. R. (1999). *We can't teach what we don't know: White teachers, multiracial schools.* New York: Teachers College Press.

McIntosh, P. (1990). White privilege: Unpacking the invisible knapsack. *Independent School, 49*(2), 31–36.

Lake, R. (Medicine Grizzlybear). (1990, September). An Indian father's plea. *Teacher Magazine, 1,* 20–23.

Paley, V. G. (1995). *Kwanzaa and me: A teacher's story.* Cambridge, MA: Harvard University Press.

West, C. (1993). *Race matters.* New York: Vintage.

Steele, C. M. (1992, April). Race and the schooling of Black Americans. *The Atlantic Monthly, 269,* 6.

CULTURAL PORTRAIT

Background

Diversity is one of the most pressing issues facing teachers today and probably one of the least understood and discussed. Too many times we make initial assumptions about people based on some distinguishing characteristic such as skin color, sex, age, physical ability, clothing, or the neighborhood in which they live. When we engage these stereotypes, we simultaneously (a) group many individuals into some kind of unified block because we believe they all see the world in the same way, (b) limit our ability to see the person as an individual because we cannot get past distinguishing characteristics and all the meanings we attach to them, and (c) position the individual as the Other, someone who is fundamentally different from us because of some physical or social marker. One resulting problem with these assumptions is the construction of boundaries that limit our expectations of whole groups of individuals and in the same instance, limit our own.

Activity

This exercise requires you to conduct a series of interviews with a person who you believe is culturally different from yourself. On concluding your interviews, you should prepare a written and/or oral narrative in which you present your informant as you came to know him or her through your interactions and present an analysis of your presuppositions concerning this individual.

Phase One: The Interview. First and foremost, your informant must be guaranteed anonymity, and strict ethical considerations of human research must be followed. Your school will have specific guidelines you should follow. You will want to take notes during this time with your informant. The use of a portable audio or video recorder would be most beneficial in capturing the entirety of the interview as well as the inflections and emotions of the informant. You must, however, follow the rules of your institution regarding this method of data gathering. At the very least, you should have written permission of the individual prior to the use of any recording medium.

You should spend time discussing such topics as (but not limited to) childhood, friends, family, goals, schooling and other forms of education, leisure activities, dating, language, church/religion, work, politics, personal points of view on contemporary issues, or any other topic your informant wishes to discuss. You are attempting to understand the world as seen through the eyes of your informant.

During your conversations, identify the cultural contexts from which this individual constructs a world view different from your own. Your intent is to identify and clarify specific cultural perspectives that provide particular meanings for events that have occurred in this person's life. In other words, it is not sufficient to simply identify what happened to your informant; your goal is to relate how and why your informant understood those events in a particular way. For instance, your informant participated in voter registration activities during the 1960s. What did that mean to this person? Why did your informant engage in this potentially dangerous activity? What was it about that era that inspired such actions on the part of so many diverse individuals?

Phase Two: The Narrative. Once the interviews are completed, you should produce a narrative to share with your classmates. This should be more than a simple transcription of the interview. You should present both a portrait of the informant's world and an analysis of your preconceptions. The bulk of the narrative will address your portrait of the informant and his or her world. In doing so, you must first clarify the cultural contexts central to the informant so that we might understand why the informant sees the world in this unique manner. Using excerpts from the interview material helps us to understand how the informant views the world and what factors might have led to those particular perspectives.

With the limitations of space or time, you will not be able to use all the material you collected in the interview. Therefore, your responsibility is to edit the material down to a manageable amount. This edited product should be broad enough to present an adequate portrait of the individual and limited enough to provide for depth of presentation. The narrative should develop in a unified manner without digression. The closing section of the narrative should address your own subjective preconceptions concerning the informant and how these changed or were reinforced during the interview.

Reflective Narrative

Why did you label this individual as being culturally different from yourself in the first place? Were these differences borne out under investigation, or did the commonalties of your experiences mitigate the differences you assumed

existed? Were your assumptions based on stereotypes? How has this experience changed the way in which you look at other people who might appear to be different from yourself? How might this exercise have an important impact on your future work as a teacher?

Related Readings

Berlak, A. (1999). Teaching and testimony: Witnessing and bearing witness to racisms in culturally diverse classrooms. *Curriculum Inquiry, 29,* 99–127.

Estola, E. (2003). Hope as work—Student teachers constructing their narrative identities. *Scandinavian Journal of Educational Research, 47,* 181–203.

Ladson-Billings, G. (1994). *The dreamkeepers: Successful teachers of African American children.* San Francisco: Jossey-Bass.

McIntosh, P. (1988). White privilege: Unpacking the invisible knapsack. *Independent School, 49*(2), 31–36.

Romo, H., & Falbo, T. (1996). *Latino high school graduation: Defying the odds.* Austin: The University of Texas Press.

NOTES

[1]See Palmer, P. (1998). *Courage to teach: Exploring the inner landscape of a teacher's life.* San Francisco: Jossey-Bass. See also, Goodlad, J. (2004). *Romances with schools.* New York: McGraw-Hill.

[2]Britzman, D. (1986). Cultural myths in the making of a teacher: Biography and social structure in teacher education. *Harvard Educational Review, 56,* 442–256.

[3]Frank, C. R., & Uy, F. L. (2004). Ethnography for teacher education. *Journal of Teacher Education, 55*(3), 269.

[4]McNergney, R. F., & Herbert, J. M. (1995). *Foundations of education: The challenge of professional practice.* Boston: Allyn & Bacon.

[5]Cain, M. (2001). Ten qualities of the renewed teacher. *Phi Delta Kappan, 82,* 702–709.

[6]David, T. (2000). Teacher mentoring: Benefits all around. *Kappa Delta Pi Record, 36,* 134–136.

[7]Scherer, M. (Ed.). (2003). *Keeping good teachers*. Alexandria, VA: Association for Supervision and Curriculum Development.

[8]Parashar, A. (n.d.). Teaching kids—UGH!! (… and what I learned from it). Retrieved December 13, 2004, from http://www.howtoadvice.com/TeachingKids

[9]Ben-Peretz, M., & Schonmann, S. (2000). *Behind closed doors: Teachers and the role of the teachers' lounge*. Albany: State University of New York Press.

[10]Britzman, D. (1986). Cultural myths in the making of a teacher: Biography and social structure in teacher education. *Harvard Educational Review, 56*, 442–456.

[11]This exercise is adapted from Peason, D. (1989). *The natural home book*. New York: Firestone Books, p. 172.

[12]See especially McLaren, P. (1989). *Life in schools: An introduction to critical pedagogy in the foundations of education*. New York: Longman.

Section 2

Regulating the "Schooled" Body

INTRODUCTION

From its inception, one of the primary goals of schooling has been to transmit to the young the values, beliefs, and knowledge necessary for the maintenance of a coherent social order. To achieve such order, members of a society must share some fundamental assumptions about how a society operates and the value and place of each member in that society. Before industrialization and urbanization, it was assumed that the church, family, and community would act as the primary socialization agents for children. However, as the influence of these institutions waned in the late 19th century, schools emerged as the primary agent of socialization with the responsibility of teaching students the fundamental principles necessary for survival in the new corporate political economy. Those principles included cooperation, obedience to authority, conformity, compliance, and discipline. To assume this new role, the school was faced with a unique problem of how a small group of adults might teach a large group of socially and ethnically diverse children both academic skills and the social principles necessary for survival in an increasingly competitive world.

Schools responded to this problem in a variety of ways: a de-emphasis on the individual and an emphasis on universalism (i.e., the uniform treatment of individuals as members of a collective entity); an emphasis on the physical control of bodies, time, and space (i.e., school rules, regulations, and policies controlling how students move, sit, eat, sleep, play, etc.); the development of multiple levels of supervision and bureaucratic control to regulate what constitutes "normal" behavior in school; and the separation of the school from the world outside of school.

The early 20th-century schools borrowed from industry the theory of scientific management to create schools that were efficient both in their organization and operation. This emulation is well illustrated in the following quote written by Cubberly in 1916:[1]

> Our schools are, in a sense, factories in which the raw products (children) are to be shaped and fashioned into products to meet the various demands of life. The specifications for manufacturing come from the demands of twentieth century civilization, and it is the business of the school to build its pupils according to the specifications laid down. This demands good tools, specialized machinery, continuous measurement of production to see it is according to specifications, the elimination of waste in manufacture, and large variety in the output. (p. 338)

Juxtaposed against this goal of preparing students for the world of work was the school's goal of separating itself from the outside world. Ironically, schools sought to prepare students for life while removing them from life.[2] In many urban areas, the philosophy of schooling that emerged by the early 20th century was that the school was a superior substitute for both families and work. This separation of the public (the school) from the private (the home) manifested itself in numerous ways from the design of school buildings[3] to the prohibition of immigrant students speaking their home language in school.

Undeniably, the schools of today closely resemble the schools of yesterday. Indeed, many would argue that schools in the 21st century continue to operate on a factory model. The student

17

is the worker, the teacher the supervisor, the administrators the management, the school board the chief executive officers, and the public the stockholders of the enterprise. In most schools, bells still dictate movement. Reminiscent of the assembly line, classrooms are typically organized in straight rows that deter students from getting off task. School days are predictable, with the school schedule controlling the minds and bodies of teachers and students. Additionally, many schools in the 21st century continue to disenfranchise themselves from the worlds of parents, communities, and pressing social issues.

Living in a postindustrial world, we must wonder if this antiquated factory model is the most appropriate for schools today. If not, why do the schools of the early 21st century seem almost identical to the schools of the early 20th century? The first exercise in this section, seating arrangements, asks you to think seriously about how the physical structure of most classrooms resemble a factory. The next two exercises, The Sick Building/Classroom Syndrome and Reading the Physical Structure of the School, focus on the larger structure of the school. Here the greater educational environment is taken into account, revealing how windows (or the lack thereof), landscaping, parking lots, and ventilation systems, to name a few, affect the experiences of students in school. The fourth exercise looks at how teachers organize and control space in individual classrooms.

In the next part of this section, Regulating the "Schooled" Body, we explore the policies and practices for controlling the bodies of students and teachers. Foucault[4] argued that modern institutions (e.g., the army, the school, the prison, and the hospital) function to inscribe bodies in specific ways. One result of such regulatory practices in our society is the production of docile bodies. Bartky[5] described how these practices function in a school:

> The student, then, is enclosed within a classroom and assigned to a desk he cannot leave; his ranking in the class can be read off the position of his desk in the serially ordered and segmented space of the classroom itself.... The student must sit upright, feet upon the floor, head erect; he may not slouch or fidget; his animate body is brought into a fixed correlation with the inanimate desk.[5] (p. 64)

Because a large number of students must be controlled by a small number of adults, crowd control becomes an unstated goal of most schools. Consequently, schools adopt certain policies and procedures for regulating student movement and student talk. Walking to the cafeteria in a straight line, using the restroom only at specified times, eliminating recess at the elementary level, and raising your hand to talk in class are all examples of how schools assume the power to regulate students' bodies. Such regulation of movement and talk is not restricted just to the students at a school, for teachers are often subjected to similar forms of regulation and surveillance. For example, teachers may eat, drink, and use the restroom only at certain times and may not have access to outside communication during the work day.

In addition to the overt strategies employed in school to control movement and speech, the bodies of both teachers and students are also regulated by "micropractices of regulation."[6] These are the unstated, often subtle, regulatory practices (e.g., teacher talk, classroom dynamics, differentiated enforcement of rules, formal and informal rewards) that shape what constitutes appropriate classed, raced, gendered, and age-related behavior. For example, certain practices (e.g., the absence in sex education classes of the topic of female sexual desire) operate at school either to control or dismiss female sexuality. Other micropractices of regulation (e.g., the assumption that couples who attend a school dance will be of the opposite sex) may send powerful antihomosexual messages.

In the fifth and sixth exercises in this section, Regulating the Female Body and Regulating the Male Body, we explore the regulatory practices in schools that seek to normalize what constitutes appropriate gendered behavior. In the next exercise, Regulating the Teacher Body, we look at how teachers also are subjected to policies of regulation. In Compulsory Heterosexuality in Schools, we examine how schools enforce the code of heterosexuality. In the exercise Dress Codes, we redirect attention to how schools literally control the bodies of students through the enforcement of dress codes. The exercises in this part of section 2 will help you gain the distance necessary to view the "schooled body" from a fresh (and perhaps different) perspective.

In the last 4 exercises of section 2, we ask you to examine and reflect on how deviancy is defined and managed in schools today. Because a primary goal of school has been and continues to be the maintenance of a particular social order, schools operate in both implicit and explicit ways to uphold what are considered to be normative values and beliefs. However, many critics of today's schools argue that in its role as a normalization agent, school is an inherently hostile place for those students and teachers who do not share the values and beliefs of White, able-bodied, heterosexual, Protestant, middle-class society. Often students who deviate from these norms are labeled by their school as being abnormal, deviant, or at risk. For example, girls who engage in physical fighting are often treated much more harshly than boys who fight because these girls are perceived as exhibiting abnormal feminine behavior. In many schools, parents who object to the daily ritual of prayers being said on the intercom are viewed by teachers and administrators as troublemakers.

Undeniably, schools devote much of their time and energy to controlling deviant behavior. Typically, at schools, deviancy of any kind is not acceptable. It wreaks havoc on the school's managerial insistence on compliance and control. Thus, schools enact certain policies, practices, and punishments seeking to ensure that students will act in normal ways. Of course, many students resist the school's attempt to prescribe what is considered normative behavior.

In Rituals of Schooling, we provide you a framework for exploring how the daily rituals of an entire school (e.g., pep rallies every Friday at 3 p.m.) and of individual classrooms function to define what constitutes appropriate behavior in school. In Fighting Violence, we ask you to look at how schools have responded to the alarming (and contradictory) reports about violence in schools, particularly in the aftermath of several highly publicized school shootings in the late 1990s. In the last two exercises, Taking Control of the Classroom and School Punishment, we allow you the opportunity to examine the elaborate system for disciplining and punishing students at your host school.

```
┌─────────────────────────────────────────────────────────────┐
│  Name ────────────────────── Course/Section ──────────────── │
│                                                                │
│  Observation Site ──────────────── Subject ───────────────── │
│                                                                │
│  Date ──────────── Other Information ─────────────────────── │
└─────────────────────────────────────────────────────────────┘
```

SEATING ARRANGEMENTS*

Background

According to the educational historian Cuban,[7] a major change that occurred in the organization of American classrooms during the 20th century has been the acquisition of movable desks, chairs, and tables. However, despite the pleas of educational reformers from John Dewey to Theodore Sizer to eliminate rows (thereby encouraging group-centered learning), the most prevalent classroom configuration continues to be desks neatly aligned in rows facing the chalkboard (or dry board) and the teacher. Although many teachers adopt this spatial arrangement simply because "it's the way classrooms have always been," the message behind such a configuration clearly indicates that teachers are to be in control (they look down on their students sitting in chairs) and students are to be docile, quiet, compliant, and still as they look up to the teacher who will direct their movement as well as their thoughts.

Activity

1. Diagram the seating arrangements for students and teacher. On the same diagram, provide additional details on other seating available in the classroom (e.g., time-out chair). Use a code to label the items: A = student chairs, B = teacher desk, and so on. Indicate the race and gender of the students on the diagram.

W = White
B = Black
H = Hispanic
M = male
F = female

2. Ask the teacher how he or she makes decisions about where students will sit or what learning stations students will visit. Do they sit alphabetically? Are they allowed to sit wherever they please? Do they change seating arrangements periodically?

3. In observing the class, pay attention to patterns of students' response according to where they are placed. For example, who participates most in class discussions and activities: the students in the front or those in the back? Do the students who sit in designated time-out areas contribute to classroom discussions?

Reflective Narrative

The organization of the physical space of a classroom implicitly promotes certain values (e.g., individuation and competition). What are the values being promoted in this classroom?

Consider the following questions in formulating your response:

What features in this classroom arrangement of space enhance learning? What kind of learning does this room arrangement most promote: teacher centered, small group, large group, individualized

*Adapted from Page, J., Page, F., & Hawk, D. (1977). *A guide to systematic observation for beginning teacher education students*. Statesboro, GA: Georgia Southern University, College of Education. Mimeographed copies.

21

work? Where did the teacher place his or her desk? Why? For control? Privacy? Availability?

Do certain students seem more comfortable about approaching the teacher's desk? Why do you think this is the case? What might the teacher do to make himself or herself more available to all students?

Do you notice any patterns in the seating arrangement based on gender, race, or ability level? Is there any informal grouping that appears to be developing in the classroom by race, gender, or ability regardless of seating arrangements?

How does the physical arrangement of this classroom regulate the bodies of the students? How could this classroom be rearranged to promote a more student-centered atmosphere?

Related Readings

Dodson-Gray, E. (1994). Culture of separated desks. In F. Mengert, K. Casey, D. Liston, D. Purpel, & H. S. Shapiro (Eds.), *The institution of education* (pp. 183–190). Needham Heights, MA: Simon & Schuster.

Hastings, N. (1995). Desks and tables: The effects of seating arrangements on task engagement in primary classrooms. *Educational Research, 37*(3), 2–14.

Mayher, J., & Brause, R. (1986). Learning through teaching: Is your classroom like your grandmother's? *Language Arts, 63,* 617–620.

Novelli, J. (1997). Classroom management: Seating solutions [and] hooray for volunteers. *Instructor, 107*(2), 78–82, 84, 103.

Rieselbach, A. (1990). Building and learning. *Teachers College Record, 92,* 272–285.

THE SICK BUILDING/CLASSROOM SYNDROME: OBSERVING CLASSROOM DESIGN AND CLIMATE FACTORS

Background

Recently, workers in large downtown office buildings, shopping malls, and suburban corporate complexes have begun to report a disturbing pattern of physical ailments including headaches, fatigue, sleeplessness, eye and nose irritation, dry throat, general loss of concentration, and nausea. Follow-up studies monitoring the indoor air of these environments have found a complex mixture of pollutants including formaldehyde vapors, radon gas, carbon monoxide, sulphur dioxide, ozone, asbestos fibers, and tobacco smoke in addition to lead in old water pipes and paint. Further research has identified additional factors thought to contribute to worker fatigue and other work-related illnesses including fluorescent lighting, air that is too humid or overly dry, a buildup of positive ions, a lack of individualized control over one's personal environmental space, excessive room temperatures, closed ventilation systems, high noise levels, and poor window placement and design. This problem of indoor pollution labeled as "the sick building syndrome" is causing unforeseen and increasing dangers to our health and our environment.[8]

This sick building syndrome is also found in many modern schools. Most modern school buildings are sterile places filled with mass-produced objects often composed of and cleaned with dangerous toxic chemicals. The rugs, furniture, and wall insulation found in many schools typically are constructed of toxic synthetic materials. Furthermore, it is not uncommon in schools to have classrooms with no windows, sealed circulating systems, and air conditioners that recirculate this polluted, toxic air for days. School bathrooms often do not provide either cleanliness or adequate privacy.

Activity

The purpose of this exercise is to identify potential problems or symptoms associated with the sick building syndrome.

1. Draw a diagram of the classroom with its climatic features, giving special attention to the following:

   a. Lighting (Natural and inside? Shades? Fluorescent?)
   b. Room temperature (In degrees if possible)
   c. Ventilation system (Cross-ventilation? Cooling system? Outside door?)
   d. Noise Levels/Carpeting (Indoor/outdoor? Kind/degree?)
   e. Windows (Types? Appropriate to the climate? Cleanliness? What is the view? Window boxes? Plants? Do the windows open?)

Use a code to label the items identified (e.g., W = windows, OD = outside door, etc.). Make a map of the classroom with specific attention to its climatic features, placement, and air flow.

2. Walk through the school facility and make note of the placement of windows, doors, water fountains, and restroom facilities. Make notes

about the temperature, noise level, and lighting throughout the school. Find out if the school has had to deal with fire safety and environmental codes. Are there repeated problems with the heating and cooling systems?

3. Walk through the restroom facilities. Are there adequate numbers of bathrooms? Do bathroom stalls for both boys and girls have doors? Are both hot and cold water provided? Are paper towels, soap, and toilet tissue available? Make notes about the smell and general cleanliness of the bathrooms. Find out how often bathrooms are thoroughly cleaned.

Reflective Narrative

What do the features and design of your host school indicate to you about the teaching–learning process? What suggestions might you offer about needed changes in lighting, room temperature, noise levels, and placement of restrooms, windows, doors, and the like that would transform the school into a healthful place for learning?

How do these features affect student learning? How do these features contribute to the dehumanization and alienation of our minds and bodies? Can you think about how, in other ways, contemporary Western lifestyles are intimately bound up with the rejection and distancing of nature from our everyday lives and experiences?

Related Readings

Cooley, J., Wong, W., Jumper, C., & Straus, D. (1998). Correlation between the prevalence of certain fungi and sick building syndrome. *Occupational and Environmental Medicine, 55*, 579–584.

Grubb, D., & Diamantes, T. (1998). Is your school sick? Five threats to healthy schools. *The Clearinghouse, 71*(4), 202–207.

LaChapelle, D. (1987). *Sacred land, sacred sex: Rapture of the deep*. Durango, CO: Kivaki Press.

Pearson, D. (1989). *The natural home book*. New York: Firestone Books.

Smith, G. (1992). *Education and the environment: Learning to live with limits*. Albany: State University of New York Press.

READING THE PHYSICAL STRUCTURE OF THE SCHOOL

Background

A primary purpose of schools in the late 19th and early 20th century was to enculturate immigrants and poor Americans into the "American way of life." Consequently, schools were specifically designed to establish a separate and distinct entity from that of home and community (see the Assessing Family–School Relationships exercise in Section 4, this volume). Embedded in the physical layout of most schools today is the belief that the school is a separate sphere from the outside world. This is most evident in such features as classrooms with no windows and tinted doors that prevent one from seeing what is going on in the world outside the school. However, numerous other features in the design of the school send a clear message to "outsiders" (e.g., parents, community members) about their place in this separate sphere.

Activity

1. Draw a diagram of the school grounds, paying special attention to the placement of landscaping, fences, playgrounds, sidewalks, athletic fields, and so forth. Where are the windows and doors located? Does a fence surround the school? Are windows and doors tinted? Where are the parking lots for students, for faculty and staff, and for visitors? Which lots have the best access to the area that contains the main office? How much area is reserved for visitor parking? Where is the playground located?

2. Sketch the layout of the main office (or wherever visitors must report). Make note of the use of counters, furniture, and office space.

Reflective Narrative

In some districts, the distance between home and school manifests itself most obviously in the forced bussing of students who often attend facilities miles from their neighborhoods. However, this message that the school will be a separate sphere from the rest of the world is also made clear in numerous other ways, from the design of the building to the placement of furniture in the office to the use of space.

There exist many instances of schools that have been too successful in making the separation and now are reaching out with such programs as community partnerships. Many schools are trying to make their schools more inviting places for the larger community, yet the tension still remains between bringing the "right" people in (e.g., parents and influential businesspeople) and keeping the "wrong" people out (e.g., community members engaged in violence or drug activity).

What message does the school you are observing send to nonschool people by its physical layout? Does it most resemble a hospital, a prison, a mall, or a home? How might your host school be fundamentally redesigned so that nonschool personnel could be more involved in the schooling of children?

Related Readings

Barta, J., & Winn, T. (1996). Involving parents in creating anti-bias classrooms. *Children Today, 24*(1), 28–31.

Epstein, J. (1995). School/family/community partnerships. *Phi Delta Kappan, 76,* 701–712.

Strickland, R. (1994). Designing the new American school: Schools for an urban neighborhood. *Teachers College Record, 96,* 32–57.

Viadero, D. (1995). Designs for change (architectural students at MIT reconfigure the traditional school). *Teacher Magazine, 6*(4), 19–21.

TEACHER MOVEMENT IN THE CLASSROOM*

Background

The movement of a teacher in the classroom is much less restricted than that of students. However, like students, teachers must negotiate the movement of their bodies within a confined space and within established rules of school culture relating to appropriate and inappropriate use of the body. For example, certain schools might frown on a teacher sitting comfortably cross-legged on top of his or her desk, whereas other schools might discourage a teacher from sitting at his or her desk for more than 5 minutes.

Activity

Sketch a seating chart. During a teacher-directed discussion, use a line to show teacher movement in the class. If the teacher stays in one place for longer than 1 minute, draw a circle at that spot and record the number of minutes.

Reflective Narrative

Does the teacher move but stay in front of the room (i.e., stage movement vs. boundary movement)? Does the teacher move among the students? Does the teacher movement seem to enhance learning? Is teacher movement used for classroom control? How?

Does the teacher have physical contact with the students? What kind? What facial expressions does the teacher have and do the students have? What arm movements does the teacher use? Do they enhance or distract from learning? Is there eye-to-eye contact? Does the teacher's posture and head movements enhance learning or indicate enthusiasm?

Do students move in the classroom? For what purposes?

Related Readings

Cannon, L. (1990). Fostering positive race, class, and gender dynamics in the classroom. *Women's Studies Quarterly, 18*, 126–134.

Csikszentmihalyi, M., & Csikszentmihalyi, I. (1990). *Flow: The psychology of optimal experience.* New York: HarperCollins.

Miller, J. P. (1993). Movement and education. In *The holistic teacher* (pp. 81–93). Toronto, Ontario, Canada: Ontario Institute for Student in Education.

Palmer, P. J. (1993). *To know as we are known: Education as a spiritual journey.* San Francisco: Harper & Row.

Sheehan, G. (1978). *Running and being.* New York: Warner Books.

*Adapted from Page, J., Page, F., & Hawk, D. (1977). *A guide to systematic observation for beginning teacher education students.* Statesboro, GA: Georgia Southern University, College of Education, mimeographed copies.

REGULATING THE FEMALE BODY

Background

Although the meritocratic rhetoric of schooling may pronounce that biological differences have no noticeable impact on the educational opportunities available to boys and girls, girls are consistently shortchanged in schools because of the cultural and social expectations that shape gender and function to regulate appropriate feminine behavior.[9] One primary way in which the school operates to define what is considered appropriate behavior is through the micropractices of regulation that control and contain femininity and female sexuality.

Activity

The following exercises are designed to interrogate the micropractices of regulation that shape normative femininity in the particular school you are observing:

1. Obtain a copy of the dress code for students. Identify those items that are female specific. What messages are being sent about how females should look and act? What are the rules governing the use of purses, makeup, brushes, hairspray, jewelry, and perfume in school?

2. Observe a sex education class or a meeting on human sexuality. Compare how male sexuality and female sexuality are being presented. Is homosexuality addressed? If so, is homosexuality discussed in male terms only or are women included in this discussion?

3. Observe students in the hall, in the cafeteria, in the gymnasium, and at a school activity (e.g., a sports event). How do female students express their femininity? Pay attention to the interactions between male and female students and between groups of females. What are the boundaries of physical contact? What contact is acceptable? Who usually initiates the contact?

4. Interview an administrator and/or a teacher about the school's policies about fighting. Are boys who fight treated any differently than girls who fight?

5. Interview a female student who participates in sports. Ask her how her experiences playing sports are similar to and different from those of boys. Explore with her the similarities and differences in how female and male athletes are perceived at the school. Ask her if cheerleaders and girl athletes are perceived the same at the school.

Reflective Narrative

Although seemingly innocuous, various rules and practices in school transmit a powerful message to girls about the proper way to dress, act, and be a female. What particular institutional regulations did you observe operating at your host school to contain or control femininity or female sexuality?

Typically, the gender code legitimated at schools reflects the values and beliefs of its middle-class teachers and administrators. If a girl is not White and/or not middle class, her gendered identity (as exemplified by her behavior and dress) is judged against a norm that does not necessarily reflect her own understandings of what it means to be a woman/female. Of course, female adolescents do not passively accept this dismissal of their feminine identities. How do the girls at your host school resist the school's attempts to control their femininity and female sexuality? How does such resistance cause conflict between certain students and teachers or administrators?

Related Readings

Adams, N. (1999). Fighting to be somebody: Resisting erasure and the discursive practices of female adolescent fighting. *Education Studies, 30,* 115–139.

Bettis, N., & Adams, N. (2003). The power of the preps and a cheerleading equity policy. *Sociology of Education, 76,* 128–142.

Fine, M. (1988). Sexuality, schooling, and adolescent females: The missing discourse of desire. *Harvard Educational Review, 58,* 29–53.

Tolman, D. (1994). Doing desire: Adolescent girls' struggles for/with sexuality. *Gender & Society, 8,* 324–342.

Weekes, D. (2002). Get your freak on: How Black girls sexualize identity. *Sex Education, 2,* 251–262.

REGULATING THE MALE BODY

Background

Recent attention has begun to focus on how schools participate in the perpetuation of our culture's dominant code of masculinity, which suggests that boys should be tough, rational, unemotional, and aggressive. For example, male athletes are often pushed by their coaches and peers to participate in a sporting event even when they have serious injuries. A male player who does not "suck it up" and opts not to play is often called a *wimp, fag,* or *sissy.* Note that these terms are deemed negative because of their association with femininity, homosexuality, or both.

Furthermore, schools send contradictory messages about what constitutes appropriate masculine behavior. Boxing, wrestling, and other contact sports are frequently glorified as evident in the athletic trophy cases that adorn many school halls. Yet, at school, boys who engage in unsanctioned physical contact (e.g., fighting, holding hands with other males) are suspended or even expelled from school.

Activity

1. Obtain a dress code. What rules deal specifically with male students? Is hair length specified for male students and not for female students? Is a jewelry code specified for boys but not for girls?

2. Observe a practice session for a sport with only male players (e.g., boys' basketball) or a typical workout session in the school weight room. What messages are sent to boys about their bodies and about masculinity, femininity, and sexuality? If there is time, observe a practice session with girls only. Compare and contrast the two practices.

3. Observe recess or another time when students are at play. Compare the type of activities in which boys are participating to those for girls. What part do the teachers play in encouraging boys and girls to adopt or reject traditional sex roles (e.g., does the teacher guide the female students to play at the house center and the boys at the block center?).

4. Observe a sex education class or another class that deals with human reproduction. What are boys being taught about male sexual desire and responsibility? Compare and contrast what boys and girls are being taught about their own sexuality.

Reflective Narrative

Just as female students are socialized at school to be "young ladies," male students are also taught masculine behavior in various ways. Having completed the preceding activities, describe your impression of the masculinity code operating at this school. Does this code of masculinity mesh with your own understandings about what constitutes masculine behavior?

Think back on your own school experiences. Can you recall any boys (perhaps you were one) who failed to meet the ideals of masculinity promoted at school and in society at large? How would you describe the school experiences of such boys? At your host school, did you observe any boys who deviated from the masculinity code? What were the repercussions for such "deviancy" (e.g., social ostricization)?

Related Readings

Connell, R. W. (2000). *The men and the boys*. Berkeley: The University of California Press.

Gilbert, R., & Gilbert, P. (1998). *Masculinity goes to school*. London: Routledge.

Katz, J. (1995). Reconstructing masculinity in the locker room: The mentors in violence prevention project. *Harvard Educational Review, 65,* 163–174.

Nilan, P. (2000). "You're hopeless, I swear to God:" Shifting masculinities in classroom talk. *Gender and Education, 12,* 53–68.

REGULATING THE TEACHER BODY

Background

In many schools, teachers have little say over what they will teach because this is dictated by state or district curriculum guides, standardized tests, and teacher-proof textbooks and resources. When teaching is reduced to a technical rationalist process, teachers lose much of the control they once had over not only curricular and pedagogical issues but also over daily practices of schooling. However, in many schools there is more at stake than simply the disempowering of teachers through the denial of curricular choices, for teachers are often denied control over their own physical space and bodies.

Activity

1. If one is available, examine a copy of the faculty dress code. Find out who created the dress code. Were teachers responsible for setting their own standards of dress?

2. What are the rules governing the use of copy machines, eating lunch, going to the restroom, working at school after hours, and so on? Are any of the teachers provided their own office space, telephones, bathrooms, study rooms? Are teachers given a key to the school? Are teachers allowed on the school premises during the weekend? May teachers take any school equipment home to work on projects?

3. Examine the faculty lounge. What is provided for the teachers? What must they bring from home? Does it invite one to spend time with one's peers, to socialize with others?

4. How are teachers rewarded and punished? What formal rewards are in place (e.g., teacher of the year, special parking permits, merit pay, etc.)? What are the informal rewards (e.g., best classes, best duty times, district-wide committee work, etc.)? What formal punishments (e.g., dismissal, probationary status) are in place? What informal punishments are meted out (e.g., exclusion from certain social events, assignment of worst classes, lunch or bus duty assignment)?

Reflective Narrative

Aronowitz and Giroux called for rethinking the role of teachers as that of transformative intellectuals who "take a responsible role in shaping the purposes and conditions of schooling."[10] How much responsibility do the teachers at your school take in shaping the purposes and conditions of their own school?

Compare and contrast the work of the teachers at your school to other professional groups (e.g., doctors, lawyers, engineers) regarding the regulation of their bodies, time, and professional autonomy. How do you account for these differences?

What structures both in the school and in society at large promote the regulation of teachers' bodies?

Related Readings

Apple, M. (1988). *Teachers and texts*. New York: Routledge & Kegan Paul.

Clarick, G. (1990). Public school teachers and the First Amendment: Protecting the right to teach. *New York University Law Review, 65*, 693–735.

Grumet, M. (1988). *Bitter milk: Women and teaching*. Amherst: University of Massachusetts Press.

Miller, J. (1990). *Creating spaces and finding voices*. Albany: State University of New York Press.

Million, J. (2004). Dress codes for teachers? *Education Digest, 69*(5), 59–61.

Prenni, T., & Lord, T. (1992). Comparing secondary school teacher and administration reaction to a required dress code. *Education, 112*, 579–583.

COMPULSORY HETEROSEXUALITY IN SCHOOLS

Background

Compulsory heterosexuality is embedded in the stated and unstated policies and practices at most schools. Quite simply, this means that all students are expected and presumed to be heterosexual. Through the omission of homosexuality in the curriculum and the sanctioning of heterosexual practices (e.g., proms and school dances), schools typically transmit a powerful antihomosexual message. Consequently, schools are very often hostile places for many gay and lesbian youth.

Activity

1. Does your school have an official gay and lesbian youth organization? If so, observe one of its meetings. If the school does not have an official organization, in what ways do gay and lesbian youth make themselves visible at this school?

2. Observe a sex education class or meeting on human sexuality. How is homosexuality addressed (if at all)?

3. Make a list of heterosexualized functions at the school (e.g., proms, king & queen of the valentine dance).

4. Does the school include sexual orientation in its Equal Employment Opportunity Commission statement?

5. What examples in curriculum materials, classroom discussion, and textbooks are based on the assumption that heterosexuality is normal (e.g., in stories about intimate relationships, are the people in the relationship ever of the same-sex?)?

6. Observe the centers (e.g., music, art, housekeeping, etc.) in your host classroom. Do boys gravitate toward one and girls to another? What happens when a boy participates in what is seen as a "girl center" (e.g., if a boy plays with a doll)? How do students respond? How does the teacher respond?

Reflective Narrative

The environment at most schools is often so hostile that most gay and lesbians (both students and teachers) remain closeted. Think back on your own school experiences. How were those students who were perceived to be gay (perhaps you were one of these students) treated by both teachers and students? Compare the school climate of your elementary and secondary school to the climate of the college or university you attend now. In small groups, share these comparisons.

Do you agree that schools for gay and lesbian youth are never sexually neutral, for they constantly experience the school as heterosexualized and homophobic?

35

Related Readings

Harbeck, K. (1992). *Coming out of the classroom closet: Gay and lesbian teachers and curricula.* New York: Harrington Park Press.

Leck, G. (2000). Heterosexual or homosexual? Reconsidering binary narratives on sexual identities in urban schools. *Education and Urban Society, 32,* 324–348.

Loutzenheiser, L. (1996). How schools play "smear the queer." *Feminist Teacher, 10,* 59–64.

Renold, E. (2000). "Coming out:" Gender, (hetero)sexuality and the primary school. *Gender & Education, 12,* 309–326.

Renold, E. (2003). "If you don't kiss me, you're dumped": Boys, boyfriends and heterosexualised masculinities in the primary school. *Educational Review, 55,* 179–194.

Sears, J. (1992). The impact of culture and ideology on the construction of gender and sexual identities. In J. Sears (Ed.), *Sexuality and the curriculum* (pp. 139–156). New York: Teachers College Press.

DRESS CODES

Background

Although school boards and individual schools have the right to create dress codes—both for students and teachers—these entities cannot regulate the appearance of students or teachers on the basis of popular opinion or collective perceptions. For example, a school board cannot arbitrarily enforce a dress code that prohibits males from wearing earrings simply because the school board members view such actions as abnormal masculine behavior. In fact, since *Tinker v. Des Moines School District* (1969),[11] court cases have repeatedly upheld students' rights to dress as they please as long as their appearance does not disrupt the educational process.

However, more and more schools, especially those in urban areas, have begun to adopt rigid dress codes in an attempt to curtail violence associated with gangs and consumer violence. For example, many school districts prohibit the wearing of red or blue attire because these colors are associated with gang membership. Many schools have also prohibited the wearing of expensive jewelry and clothes because numerous students who have worn such attire have been attacked (and even killed) by someone who wanted their clothes or jewelry. Hundreds of school districts in both suburban and urban areas have adopted school uniforms to try to regulate the appearance of students.

Activity

1. Obtain a copy of the dress code for both teachers and students at your school and answer the following questions: What are the restrictions about hair length, facial hair, earrings, belts, shoes, sweat pants, shorts, tattoos, and jewelry? What does the dress code say about wearing clothes that advertise products such as Nike® or Northface? What does the dress code say about wearing clothes that advertise music groups and singers, tobacco products, alcoholic beverages, or drugs? What restrictions pertain specifically to the appearance of female and male students? Are there any restrictions about wearing specific colors? Are certain types of clothing banned (e.g., clothes with rebel flags, FUBU)?

2. Policies regarding dress codes vary from school district to school district. In some districts, school boards are responsible for creating their own dress codes. Find out who was responsible for creating the dress code at your school: the school board, the principal, teachers, or a committee consisting of teachers, students, parents, and so forth. How might the makeup of those designing the dress code be reflected in the particulars established?

3. In recent years, more and more public schools have begun to use uniforms. Have uniforms been adopted at this school? If so, interview a teacher or administrator to find out why uniforms were adopted. Are the uniforms manda-

tory? What has been the response from parents and students? What influence have uniforms had on students' behavior? If the school has not adopted a uniform policy, have uniforms been discussed recently? What precipitated such a discussion? Why were uniforms ultimately rejected?

Reflective Narrative

Many would argue the dress codes and the adoption of uniforms helps to control disruptive and violent behavior and to diminish differences based on social class. However, critics of strict dress codes and uniforms argue that these regulatory mechanisms restrict individual expression. At the school you observed, does the dress code restrict the expression of individual identity or cultural identity? If so, in what ways? How do the codes affirm certain cultural identities?

Dress codes also often operate as a regulatory mechanism for what constitutes appropriate feminine and masculine behavior. In what ways, if any, did the school through its dress code regulate appropriate ways of looking and being for male and female students? How does this dress code enforce compulsory heterosexuality?

Do students have their own informal dress codes? For example, are certain groups of students identified with a particular way of dressing? How do students demonstrate resistance to the school's attempts to regulate their individual and cultural expression through dress codes and school uniforms?

In many Southern communities, wearing clothes that display the Confederate flag is prohibited. A school district in Texas prohibited its students from wearing Doc Martens® because of their association with a skinhead group. Do you think Confederate flag clothing or Doc Martens interfere with the ability of the school to function properly? Explain. Do you think schools should have a dress code? Why or why not?

Related Readings

Alvez, A. (1994). Will dress codes save our schools? *Update on Law Education, 18*(2), 9–13.

LaPoint, V., Holloman, L., & Alleyne, S. (1992). The role of dress codes, uniforms in urban schools. *NASSP Bulletin, 76,* 20–26.

Meadmore, D., & Symes, C. (1997). Keeping up appearances: Uniform policy for school diversity? *British Journal of Educational Studies, 45,* 174–186.

Mitchell, H., & Knechtle, J. (2003). Uniforms in public schools and the First Amendment: A constitutional analysis. *The Journal of Negro Education, 72,* 487–494.

RITUALS OF SCHOOLING

Background

Like other social institutions, schools and individual classrooms have their own distinct rituals comprising what is often called "school culture." Pledging allegiance to the flag, observing a moment of silent meditation, and listening to morning announcements are all rituals that are clearly associated with schools. For many people, these rituals are so ingrained in the way schools are supposed to be that they are given little thought. In many school districts, these rituals are associated with Christian practices (e.g., saying a prayer before a football game) and often violate the separation of church and state. Sometimes individuals or groups challenge such rituals (e.g., refuse to salute the flag or challenge prayer over the intercom) and by doing so are often viewed as troublemakers, "liberals," or disloyal Americans. The challenging of such rituals often leads to the establishment of new rituals that are more inclusive of all members of the student body (e.g., changing the school mascot from the Dixie Gents to the Crimson Pride).

Activity

1. What rituals begin and end the school day? Are any of these rituals associated with Christian practices (e.g., prayer)? Are other religions represented in any of these rituals? What happens to students who do not participate in these rituals? Are there any rituals that are exclusive to one school subcultural group (i.e., boys go to the first baseball game; Blacks have their own prom, etc.)?

2. Interview a teacher to discover what other school rituals exist (e.g., a pep rally every Friday afternoon during football season, an Honors banquet at the end of every school year, graduation ceremonies). How long have these rituals existed? Has anyone ever challenged them?

3. Observe the same class period for several days. What rituals exist in this classroom (e.g., lining up for the bathroom, passing out papers, going out to recess)?

Reflective Narrative

Undeniably, some school rituals infringe the individual rights of certain students, and some rituals (e.g., prayers said over the intercom) clearly violate the Constitution of the United States. Yet, rituals also serve to create a distinct school ethos and often serve as the bridge between schools and local communities. In your host school, what rituals exist that you view as bordering on a violation of individual rights or legal mandates? What rituals exist that are unique to this school? How do the rituals serve to create a feeling of belonging and community? What part does tradition play in the continuation of these rituals? Is this positive or negative?

Related Readings

Bergman, J. (1997). The modern religious objection to mandatory flag salute in America: A history and evaluation. *Journal of Church and State, 39,* 215–237.

Deever, B. (1994). Living *Plessey* in the context of *Brown*: Cultural politics and the rituals of separation. *Urban Review, 26,* 273–288.

McLaren, P. (1986). *Schooling as a ritual performance: Toward a political economy of educational symbols and gestures.* Boston: Routledge & Kegan Paul.

Tatum, B. (2003). *"Why are all the Black kids sitting together in the cafeteria?:" And other conversations about race.* New York: Basic Books.

FIGHTING VIOLENCE IN THE SCHOOLS

Background

In the late 1990s, four school shootings received tremendous media coverage, leading many to believe that schools have become increasingly violent places. In reality, the number of violent acts committed on school campuses has actually decreased. According to the Center for Disease Control national Youth Risk Behavior Survey, 6.1% of students reported bringing weapons to school. In 1991, that number was 11.8%. The number of physical fights occurring on school campuses has decreased from 16.2% in 1991 to 12.8% in 2003. Despite the facts about school violence, the number of students who miss school because they fear for their safety increased from 4.4% in 1991 to 5.4% in 2003. This increase was most significant in White, female students. To counter this image of schools as unsafe places, many schools have adopted a "get tough" approach to fighting violence. However, in many cases, this approach has not proven to be an effective antidote to violence in schools, as students and teachers continue to be victims of violence even in schools that have installed metal detectors, surveillance cameras, and on-site police officers. Consequently, more and more schools are taking a proactive approach to dealing with violence by teaching students mediation and conflict-resolution skills.

Activity

Choose at least one of the following exercises to explore how your host school has addressed the problem of violence.

1. Discover which of the following measures have been implemented in an attempt to deal with the problem of violence at the school:

_____ Surveillance cameras
_____ Metal detectors
_____ Armed part-time/full-time police officers
_____ A "lock down" facility
_____ Unarmed part-time/full-time police officers
_____ A "zero tolerance" policy for weapons
_____ Students' lockers/cars search
_____ Closed lunches
_____ Dress codes
_____ Conflict resolution programs
_____ Mentoring programs
_____ Teacher–student advisory programs
_____ Conflict resolution skills integrated into the curriculum
_____ Guest speakers that include ex-prisoners and gang members
_____ Values/character education
_____ Peace education
_____ Other: ————————————————

2. Interview an administrator to find out the effectiveness of these measures in decreasing violence in the school.

3. Interview a student about his or her perceptions of the violence-prevention measures taken at the school. Does he or she feel safer with such measures? How effective does he or she think the measures have been?

4. Obtain a map of the school. Ask students to indicate the places in their school where they do not feel safe. Are there certain places that certain students do not feel safe?

Reflective Narrative

The typical message concerning violence that is being delivered by schools is that violence must be countered with force: thus the phrase "fighting violence." Embedded in this ideology of fighting violence is the belief that schools can be made safer if they are made more secure. This heightened security, however, can foster a prison-like climate. By making schools "prisons" through the use of force and coercion to acquire obedience, the school plays a role in perpetuating the very attitudes against which it is supposedly fighting. Additionally, one must question how effective measures of force and coercion are in decreasing acts of violence at schools. Furthermore, such an ideology impacts the majority of students who are not participating in violent behavior.

What message does this school send out about violence: Violence must be countered with force or violence must be countered with an ethic of care and concern? Which philosophy do you support and why?

Some schools boast of their increased suspension, expulsion, and arrest rates since adopting get tough approaches to violence, whereas others suppress this same information. What beliefs about violence support these behaviors? Does your school present or silence such statistics? With which approach do you agree?

What alternative measures might your school take in dealing with violence?

Related Readings

Casella, R. (2003). Zero tolerance policy in schools: Rationale, consequences, and alternatives. *Teachers College Record, 105,* 872–892.

Huff, C., & Trump, K. (1996). Youth violence and gangs: School safety initiatives in urban and suburban school districts. *Education and Urban Society, 28,* 492–503.

Johnson, I. (1999). School violence: The effectiveness of a school resource officer program in a Southern city. *Journal of Criminal Justice, 27,* 173–192.

Noguera, P. (1995). Preventing and producing violence: A critical analysis of responses to school violence. *Harvard Educational Review, 65,* 189–212.

Sullivan, M. (2002). Exploring layers: Extended case method as a tool for multilevel analysis of school violence. *Sociological Methods and Research, 31,* 255–285.

Watts, I., & Erevelles, N. (2004). These deadly times: Reconceptualizing school violence by using critical race theory and disability studies. *American Educational Research Journal, 41,* 271–299.

TAKING CONTROL OF THE CLASSROOM

Background

A most often cited problem of beginning teachers is insufficient knowledge about classroom management. Thus, hundreds of workshops touting the latest gimmick for dealing with discipline problems have been created and sold to school districts. However, a growing body of research suggests that many of the discipline problems occurring in schools today are related to general student boredom, regimented classes and teachers, and ineffective teaching strategies (e.g., an overreliance on lecture). Thus, teachers often have to rely on their own intuitive knowledge about how to create and maintain a supportive learning environment that minimizes discipline problems.

Activity

Participate in the following activities to examine how student behavior and classroom management is handled in the class you are observing:

1. Observing student misbehavior: Note the kinds of student behaviors that seem to be most disruptive in the classroom that you are observing:

_____ Talking
_____ Daydreaming
_____ Shouting out answers
_____ Throwing things
_____ Hitting other children
_____ Verbal sparring
_____ Other:

When did you see most of the misbehavior occur?

_____ At the beginning of a lesson
_____ At the end of the lesson
_____ During transition times
_____ At the beginning of the day
_____ At the end of the day
_____ After lunch/recess/bathroom breaks
_____ Other: _____
_____ Other: _____
_____ Other: _____

2. Observing teacher behavior: Note the different strategies the teacher used to handle behavioral problems in the classroom. Tally the number of times the teacher uses the following strategies:

_____ Eye conduct and/or hand signal to a student
_____ Immediately send student to the principal's office
_____ Ignore the student behavior
_____ Assign the student to detention
_____ Mark student's name on the board as a warning
_____ Send a note home to a parent about the student's behavior
_____ Touch a student on the shoulder or head to redirect attention
_____ Stand close to a student

_____ Provide candy or some other kind of treat or reward

_____ Provide an academic time-out

_____ Verbally redirect a student's attention

_____ Use a strong verbal reprimand

_____ Assign punish work to be completed at home

_____ Use public humiliation

_____ Other: _____

Reflective Narrative

On the basis of these observations, what do you conclude about how the students in this class view the teacher's authority, their own self-esteem, and general rules of appropriate classroom behavior? Try to be as specific as possible with your responses.

Do you think teachers create discipline problems? Think back on your own school experiences: Did you repeatedly exhibit inappropriate behavior in the classroom? What techniques worked best in redirecting your behavior?

Comment on the following statement: "Good teachers don't have to worry about discipline."

Related Readings

Bohn, C., Roehrig, A., & Pressley, M. (2004). The first days of school in the classrooms of two more effective and four less effective primary-grade teachers. *The Elementary School Journal, 104*(4), 269–287.

Hoover, R., & Kindsvatter, R. (1997). *Democratic discipline: Foundation and practice*. Englewood Cliffs, NJ: Prentice Hall.

Horsche, P., Chen, J., & Nelson, D. (1999). Rules and rituals: Tools for creating a respectful, caring learning community. *Phi Delta Kappan, 81*, 223–228.

Purkey, W., & Strahan, D. (2002). *Inviting positive classroom discipline*. Westerville, OH: National Middle School Association.

Schimmel, D. (2003). Collaborative rule-making and citizenship education: An antidote to the undemocratic hidden curriculum. *American Secondary Education, 31*(3), 16–35.

Wasicsko, M. W., & Ross, S. (1994). How to create discipline problems. *The Clearing House, 67*, 248–251.

SCHOOL PUNISHMENT

Background

Every school has its own way of punishing students who break school rules. Typical methods include suspension (both in school and out of school), detention, corporal punishment, after-school detention, manual labor (e.g., cleaning the cafeteria), and the withholding of privileges (e.g., recess). However, in many schools, inequities exist in who gets punished, why they get punished, and the type of punishment meted.

According to a study conducted by the Office of Civil Rights,[12] Black students are 74% to 86% more likely to receive corporal punishment than White students and 54% to 88% more likely to be suspended from school. Furthermore, students in low-ability groups are punished more often than students in high-ability groups, and boys are punished more often than girls.

Activity

To learn more about the kinds of punishment used at your host school, complete at least one of the following activities:

1. Talk to a teacher or administrator to determine what punishment measures are used at this school:

_____ In-school suspension
_____ Expulsion
_____ Manual labor
_____ Withholding of privileges
_____ Writing lines, definitions, etc.
_____ Rewards
_____ Denial
_____ Out-of-school suspension
_____ Detention
_____ Time-out measures
_____ Corporal punishment
_____ Public humiliation
_____ Payment of a fine
_____ Silent lunch
_____ Other: _____

2. Obtain a student handbook. Are the punishment measures explained clearly? For example, what wrongdoings constitute automatic suspension or expulsion?

3. Find out the statistics concerning the number of suspensions and expulsions by race and gender. Observe an in-school suspension room and/or timeout room. How is it organized? What are the rules? Who oversees the students? What are the demographics of the students in this room? Talk to a teacher to determine what the academic repercussions are for students who have been suspended. For example, are students able to make up work they miss during suspension?

4. Talk to an administrator to find out what part parents play in the punishment of their children. For example, does a parent personally have to bring his or her child back to school after a suspension? Are parents given choices about what kinds of punishment their child should receive?

5. What are the rules governing the use of corporal punishment? Who administers it? Does

someone have to witness it? How hard can a person be paddled?

Reflective Narrative

Did you notice a correlation between race or gender and school punishment? If so, hypothesize why these differences exist. What might the punishment code at this school implicitly teach children about power and the use of power?

What is your personal philosophy about discipline and punishment? Will you (or do you) use corporal punishment with your own children? Do you think corporal punishment teaches children to be violent? Do you believe in the adage "spare the rod; spoil the child"? Does that adage have a place in schools?

Punishments such as suspension and expulsion actually have little impact in the deterring of most misbehavior. What alternatives might be implemented at this school to encourage more appropriate behavior?

Related Readings

Atkins, M., McKay, M., Frazier, S., Jakoboson, L., Arvanitis, P., Cunningham, T., Brown, C., & Lambrecht, L. (2002). Suspensions and detentions in an urban, low-income school: Punishment or reward? *Journal of Abnormal Child Psychology, 30,* 361–371.

Jackson, G. (1994). Promoting civility on the academic network: Crime and punishment, or the Golden Rule? *Educational Record, 75,* 29–39.

McCarthy, J. D., & Hoge, D. S. (1987). The social construction of school punishment: Racial disadvantage out of universalistic process. *Social Forces, 65,* 1101–1120.

Rothsein, S. (1984). *The power to punish: A social inquiry into coercion and control in urban schools.* Lanham, MD: University Press of America.

NOTES

[1]Cubberly, E. (1916). *Public school administration.* Boston: Houghton Mifflin, p. 338.

[2]Musgrove, F. (1964). *Youth and the social order.* Bloomington: Indiana University Press.

[3]According to Stanley Rothsein, the schools of the early 20th century were designed after the asylums prevalent at the time. See Rothsein, S. (1987). The ethics of coercion: Social practices in an urban junior high school. *Urban Education, 22,* 53–72.

[4]Foucault, M. (1979). *Discipline and punish.* New York: Vintage.

[5]Bartky, S. (1990). *Femininity and domination.* New York: Routledge, p. 64.

[6]Foucault, M. (1980). *Power knowledge: Selected interviews and other writings, 1972–1977.* Sussex, England: Harvester.

[7]Cuban, L. (1984). *How teachers taught: Constancy and change in American classrooms 1890–1980.* New York: Longman.

[8]Pearson, D. (1989). *The natural home book.* New York: Firestone Books.

[9]Sadker, M., & Sadker, D. (1994). *Failing at fairness: How our schools cheat girls.* New York: Simon & Schuster.

[10]Aronowitz, S., & Giroux, H. (1985). *Education under siege: The conservative and radical debate over schooling.* South Hadley, MA: Bergin & Garvin Publishers, p. 126.

[11]*Tinker v. Des Moines,* 393 U.S. 503 (1969).

[12]As cited in P. Noguera. (1995). Preventing and producing violence: A critical analysis of responses to school violence. *Harvard Educational Review, 65,* 189–212.

Section 3

Pedagogy and School Cultures: Issues of Race, Class, and Gender

INTRODUCTION

We dedicate this section of the book to exploring the multiple connections of schooling and how they affect teacher–student interactions, curriculum, the relation of schools to the surrounding social-historical-cultural spheres, and linkages between students and the school environment. Each set of exercises is designed to make the familiar strange. Having spent most of your lives in schools, these places are very familiar to you. Although this familiarity with patterns and processes of schooling can be comforting and might make your life as a student somewhat easier, it does lead to a kind of tunnel vision. After a while, policies, practices, and procedures become such a routine part of our lives that we stop asking why things are done and only concentrate on how things are done. For example, consider the following routine aspects of schooling and the accompanying questions that ask you to analyze school experiences often taken for granted:

- If a lively classroom discussion is taking place, does that necessarily mean that all students are participating or that all students are being treated equitably by the teacher? How about the kinds of responses given by teachers? Might there be patterns of bias that are not readily evident?
- We all know that schools teach subject content, but what about that subject content that is excluded? Does that silence send a message about the worth of that particular knowledge?

- What are the historical roots for the things we do in schools? Investigating these hidden roots might lead to surprising revelations about the cultural origins of particular practices and procedures. Knowledge about these origins might lead one to then consider whether the practices or procedures still have a place in contemporary schooling.
- Is all misbehavior a form of deviance, or might this sometimes be a form of student resistance? If so, what might students be resisting?

In other sections of this book, you have been asked to examine your own prejudices and preconceptions. Now, do your best to look around or beyond those preconceptions and examine schools and schooling. Approach this section with the eyes of a child and try to see schools as something completely different from what you assume them to be. We begin with an overview of the study to follow.

The Hidden Curriculum: Problems and Possibilities

- Textbook analysis
- Moral messages in everyday instruction

Hidden curriculum, a term used in educational studies for approximately the last 30 years, refers to any number and variety of practices or relationships that occur without the expressed knowledge of the teacher and the students.[1] One might wonder how hidden aspects of schooling get hidden in the first place. It is simply because no one sees what is happening. No one thinks to look. Much of what we do in classrooms is based on unreflective thought, and our actions are often guided by assumptions taken for granted about society and people (ideology). These assumptions can create a kind of blindness. To seek out hidden curricula requires you to move beyond the blindness to engage the processes of schooling from a different perspective.

The ability to seek out hidden curricula is predicated on one's capacity to see through the fog of "common sense" and demands recognition that engaging the hidden curricula must be approached as a moral and ethical exercise. Once a hidden curriculum is uncovered, several options exist for the education worker. It might be ignored, modified by changing the practices that bring it about, abolished, or embraced.[2] The decision to act or not to act, to modify or celebrate, must be understood as having its roots in one's personal matrix of values. The manner in which one teacher reacts to the presence of a hidden curriculum may be vastly different from that of another due to dissimilarities in each individual's set of value beliefs. Therefore, a critical part of choosing options is to have a firm sense of one's own normative position. Simply stated, you need to know what you believe and why you believe it. Then you must recognize that those beliefs are going to guide your actions in the classroom and beyond, consciously and/or unconsciously.

Understanding your beliefs and the concrete effects of those beliefs is the first step. You must then weigh out the possible consequences of your actions. Again, these consequences must be defined in terms of what you believe to be in the best interest of those involved. These consequences must be seen in terms of their concrete effects matched against other possible courses of action. In reflecting on these things, we are once more placed in a normative realm of subjective decision making. Clarity of values, purposes, and consequences are essential to this process.

Once the decision has been made and acted on, we have the additional responsibility of monitoring the results of our actions and of modifying or amplifying according to our ethical referents. In summary, the process of dealing with a hidden curriculum requires more than a simple awareness of its presence. We must have reflective awareness, inner vision, and a firm set of normative referents with which to guide and ultimately evaluate our actions.

Thus it is with education work at large. With the pervasive presence of hidden consequences in the schooling process, nearly every decision we make must be guided by our framework of beliefs and values. To choose actions based on "objective" criteria is to beg the question and to engage in uninformed educational practice.

Teacher–Student Dialogical Processes

- Teacher wait time
- Brain-compatible classroom
- Classroom dialogue 1: Frequency
- Classroom dialogue 2: Content
- Classroom characteristics and climate

This segment of the section explores the multitude of dialogic interactions that occur between teachers and students in the regular classroom setting. These interactions are an embedded part of daily classroom life and simultaneously take place at multiple levels: open and covert, verbal and nonverbal, spoken and silent. The Teacher Wait-Time exercise explores the role of silence in the dialogic processes of learning and the manner in which these structured spaces can be used (intentionally and/or unintentionally) to send powerful messages to students. The Brain-Compatible Classroom exercise also explores the larger communicative context of the classroom and the manner in which this context might inhibit or advance the construction of more effective learning opportunities.

The driving concept behind these exercises is voice. By *voice* we mean the manner in which the integrated sum of our experiences, our cultural intersections, and our multiple identities come together to form our unique patterns of communicative engagement with the social and physical worlds around us. Open and equitable dialogue is critical to the establishment and perpetuation of a classroom site in which the multiple voices of all students are legitimated and nurtured.

Part of the criteria for a successful, healthy, and democratic social community is the establishment of open and equitable dialogue in which all members have both equal access to and equitable hearings in the social conversations of that community. In the classrooms of public schools, students begin to learn how such communities are established. To some degree, the future success or failure of an equitable social order may be impacted by these early contexts in the public schools. If students learn that their voices and perspectives are both legitimate and necessary for the microcommunity of the classroom to function, they probably are more likely to carry these lessons of participation with them into the real world. However, those students whose voices and perspectives are continually silenced may be less likely to participate in the conversations of their communities and may withdraw from active citizenship in the larger social world. Widespread and systematic disenfranchisement of this sort then becomes the bane of a participatory democracy and leads to isolation and retreat from public life.

The final three exercises in this segment of the section ask you to examine the manner in which dialogue is constructed and managed in your host site. Is there an open and equitable context wherein all students may freely participate? Do all students have the same opportunities or dialogic communion? Is the classroom set up in a way that provides multiple learning opportunities and equal access to the production of knowledge and meaning? This section is about more than observing who talks to whom. It is about investigating how the roots of democratic participation are nurtured in a free society.

Students' Interests and Dilemmas

- Shadowing a student
- Student resistance
- Student ridicule and harassment

For students, schools are more than work sites or places of learning: They are the major social center of their lives. Although most educational training is concerned with the cognitive aspects of school life, there are other aspects that occur outside the classroom walls. The focus of these exercises is on beginning to see the world from the eyes of the student. You might argue that you were a student most recently and that these experiences are fresh in your mind. True, but these are your experiences. Do other students see the school world differently than you do? This is an opportunity to find out. This also is an opportunity to explore the multiple realities of schooling that get constructed by all the participants. Because a portion of student time is spent outside the direct gaze of the teacher in the classroom, it is important to recognize and consider how the actions within these temporal spaces contribute to the entire process of doing schooling.

TEXTBOOK ANALYSIS

Background

Studies have shown that the single force driving most classroom instruction is the textbook.[3] This is true at all levels of education from elementary through university. The textbook is the source, the "fount of truth and knowledge," unimpeachable, and presumably, accurate and neutral. The textbook is the curriculum guide: It controls our learning calendar and dominates our approach to teaching. This probably comes as no surprise to you because you have read textbooks for years. In fact, you are reading a criticism of textbooks in a textbook at this moment, and this probably seems perfectly normal. That is precisely the point. We have come to accept the overwhelmingly powerful influence of textbooks with nary a second thought. Textbooks are one of the taken-for-granted aspects of organized education in this country.[4]

Activity

When teachers are asked to evaluate texts, they usually are given a set of guiding questions such as these: Is the reading level appropriate?, Are the chapters arranged in a logical manner?, Are the illustrations appropriate and interesting?, Is the information accurate?, Is the cover durable?, Are the ancillary materials complete?, and so forth. These are mechanical questions. This exercise challenges you to look differently at texts.

To begin, obtain a copy of the primary text used in the classroom in which you are observing. If secondary texts are available, use them for comparative purposes. If a teacher's manual is available, inspect that also. Consider the following questions:

1. Where does knowledge originate? How does the textbook address this question? Does it tell students to ask the teacher or to discover for themselves? Does it challenge students to create their own knowledge or does it simply tell, transmitting knowledge to students as passive receivers?

2. Who is the authority: the book, the teacher, the student, or some combination?

3. What hidden messages are embedded in the textbook? Are there obvious gender, racial, or class-specific biases or stereotypes? This can be tricky at first, but look at stories, narratives, examples, and illustrations. These can be powerful media for transmitting particular messages to the unwitting reader.

4. Examine the table of contents. What is missing? It is not so much what knowledge is missing as what perspectives are missing.

5. What could or should have been included? What would have made this text more complete, more diverse, and more representative?

Reflective Narrative

Did you consider applying these questions to texts that you are using in other classes? What about the text you are reading now? What about a "world history" text that might ignore a significant portion of the planet by focusing on Western

Europe? How many economic systems other than capitalism are examined?

As a teacher in your own classroom, how might you supplement the texts you examined? Using available technology (e.g., World Wide Web), construct alternatives for traditional texts. Draw up some specific examples and discuss them with your host teacher.

Related Readings

Altbach, P. G., Kelly, G. P., Petrie, H. G., & Weis, L. (Eds.). (1991). *Textbooks in American society: Politics, policy and pedagogy.* Albany: State University of New York Press.

Apple, M. W. (1986). *Teachers and texts.* New York: Routledge & Kegan Paul.

Ball, D. L., & Feiman-Nemser, S. (1988). Using textbooks and teachers' guides: Dilemmas for beginning teachers and teacher educators. *Curriculum Inquiry, 83*(4), 401–423.

Coser, L. A., Kadushin, C., & Powell, W. W. (Eds.). (1982). *Books: The culture and commerce of publishing.* Chicago: University of Chicago Press.

Jackson, P. W., & Harouteman-Gordon, S. (Eds.). (1990). From Socrates for software: The teacher as text and the text as teacher. *Eighty-eighth yearbook of the National Society for the Study of Education, part I.* Chicago: NSSE.

| Name _____ | Course/Section _____ |
| Observation Site _____ | Subject _____ |
| Date _____ Other Information _____ |

MORAL MESSAGES IN EVERYDAY INSTRUCTION

Background

There has been continuing controversy stimulating great public debate about the role of morals in public education. Some claim that schools should simply transmit knowledge and facts without including morals. Others seek to proselytize from their particular religious perspective and view the loss of school prayer as the demise of Western culture.

For others, this way of framing the debate misses the mark. Indeed, these educators claim that it is impossible to teach without sending moral messages both overtly and covertly. According to these educators, every time teachers encourage, advocate, or demand that students "behave," they are teaching morals.

Activity

Use the chart in Fig. 3.1 to make note of all of the moral statements in the classroom. In the first column, write the teacher's comments that contain a stated or implied "should" or "ought." For example, "Raise your hand before speaking," or "Wait your turn." In the second column, write responses from students to the statements. For example, "Student raised hand while speaking, and was acknowledged by teacher," or "Student returned to desk."

At the end of your observation period, count up the number of should/ought statements made by the teacher. How many of these comments were made? Next, calculate what percentage of the class time was "taken up" with moral messages.

Reflective Narrative

Now, look more closely at the statements you have gathered from your teacher. What are the moral messages being taught? How are students being encouraged to treat one another? What place does self hold for each student? (For example, when a student raises his or her hand and is not called on, what message does this convey for that student's self esteem? How long should one wait to be recognized?)

What are the further implications of your findings? Do you agree that should/ought statements carry moral messages? Based on this exercise, what do you think are the moral messages being sent most often to children in public schools? Are these morals with which you can agree? Why or why not?

Related Readings

Beck, C. (1995). Postmodernism, ethics and moral education. In W. Kohli (Ed.), *Critical conversations in philosophy of education* (pp. 127–136). New York: Routledge.

Noddings, N. (1992). *The challenge to care in schools: An alternative approach to education.* New York: Teachers College Press.

Purpel, D. (1989). *The moral and spiritual crisis in education: A curriculum for justice and compassion in education.* New York: Bergin & Garvey.

Purpel, D. (1999). *Moral outrage in education.* New York: Peter Lang.

Comments of Teachers	Comments/Responses of Students

FIG. 3.1.   Moral Messages in Everyday Instruction worksheet (reproduce as needed).

TEACHER WAIT TIME[5]

Background

Most people believe that speech is the most effective way to communicate thoughts and ideas to others. Speaking is, in fact, the most commonly used form of communication in our society. However, what we do not say, or more specifically, the interspaces between what we do say, are also powerful components of the communication process. However, like many other aspects of teaching, we neither fully realize nor explore the effects generated by this subtle nonverbal aspect of communication.

In formal training, most preservice teachers are taught the art of questioning. One part of the questioning process is *wait time:* the time between the question and either the student response or your follow-up. Many teachers vaguely recommend some general amount of wait-time (until the student starts to get uncomfortable or is clearly perplexed), but we focus here on wait time as a specific and powerful communicative tool that speaks through its structured silences. Embedded in wait time are subtle clues about your judgments of a student's abilities and your expectations of individuals and groups. For example, the more time you allow a student to mull through a question, the more you trust his or her ability to answer that question without getting flustered.

As a rule, the practice of prompting is not a problem. Giving support and helping students reason through difficult conundrums is part of being an effective teacher. The problem emerges, however, if you consistently distribute wait time inequitably. For instance if female students are consistently given significantly less wait time than are male students, a powerful prejudicial message might be sent to the class as a whole about the perceived abilities of these individuals.

Activity

Phase 1. Figure 3.2 is a chart on which to record your observations about teacher wait-time. You may need a stopwatch for this exercise, although any clock that indicates seconds will be sufficient (and unobtrusive). In looking at the chart, you will notice the following nomenclature for recording your observations.

M	F	Wait Time
✓		:25
	✓	X
✓		:13

When the teacher asks a student a question, start your watch and check whether the student is a female or a male student. If the student speaks before the teacher, place an X in the Wait-Time box. If the teacher speaks before the student, stop your watch and write down the elapsed time. Do not expect to catch every interchange, especially in classes with lively questioning and a fast pace. However, over an extended period of time, patterns will begin to emerge.

Phase 2. Talk with male and female students from the classes you observed and ask them how they like those particular subjects. See if they mention the teacher's attitude in their comments.

Reflective Narrative

What patterns did you discover? If the teacher was equitable in his or her questioning, ask why and how questioning is part of his or her pedagogy. Are there other aspects to the class that contradict or support your wait-time observations? How might you teach yourself to be more aware of wait time in your own teaching?

Related Readings

Freed, A. F. (1992). We understand perfectly: A critique of Tannen's view of cross-sex communication. In K. Hall, M. Bucholtz, & B. Moonwoman (Eds.), *Locating power: Proceedings of the Second Berkeley Women and Language Conference 1* (pp. 144–152). Berkeley, CA: Berkeley Women and Language Group.

Ozerk, K. (2001). Teacher–student verbal interaction and questioning, class size and bilingual students' academic performance. *Scandinavian Journal of Educational Research, 45,* 353–367.

Sadker, M., Sadker, D., & Long, L. (1989). Gender and educational equality. In J. A. Banks & C. A. M. Banks (Eds.), *Multicultural education: Issues and perspectives* (pp. 105–123). Boston: Allyn & Bacon.

Tannen, D. (1990). *You just don't understand: Men and women in conversation.* New York: Ballantine.

Weikel, B. (1995). "Girlspeak" and "boyspeak:" Gender differences in classroom discussion. In J. S. Kleinfeld & S. Yerian (Eds.), *Gender tales: Tensions in the schools* (pp. 7–11). New York: St. Martin's Press.

F	M	Wait Time	F	M	Wait Time	F	M	Wait Time

FIG. 3.2. Wait-Time worksheet (reproduce as needed).

BRAIN-COMPATIBLE CLASSROOM EXERCISE

Background

Recent findings in neuroscience are important for the field of education. Teachers are often so busy with the mechanics of teaching that they forget that "the brain is the organ of learning."[6] In our teacher preparation programs, we spend considerable time learning how to plan a lesson and how to deliver it but devote little or no time to learning about how the brain functions. We now know a great deal about how the brain is impacted by enriched environments, threats, food, stress, feedback, and hundreds of other stimuli, but how does it all relate to the classroom?

The brain-based or brain-compatible classroom approach is based on current research in neuroscience that suggests how our brain naturally learns best. This approach is not a panacea for all pedagogical problems, but it does provide a research-based and biologically driven framework for understanding learning. To learn better, we must first better understand the human brain.

Neurons are the basic cells of the brain. Most neurons form connections with other neurons rather than function independently and randomly. In this way, the brain constructs neural networks. These networks tend to form and reform in a set order. Once a neural network is formed, it has a tendency to reform again and again. In much the same way as people at a crowded party tend to gravitate toward individuals they already know, neurons gravitate toward familiar neurons—those that have previously been in associated networks.

Findings such as these from the field of neuroscience indicate that certain classroom practices and activities should be more successful than others. The primary indication is that learning occurs best when ideas are placed in context so that students can connect new learning with previously established neural networks. Thus, subject matter in schools should be relevant to real-life concerns of learners. As real-life concerns are transformed into classroom projects, the false separation between real life and classroom life dissolves, and students encounter education in an integrated fashion.

In addition to working with students' neural networks, educational practices should allow students to choose a topic, the method of addressing the topic, and the manner of demonstrating an understanding of the topic, thus feeding the students' natural *epistemic hunger* or the genetically driven imperative to form neural networks.[7] Therefore, the more students discover and simultaneously create neural networks, the more they desire to learn.

Activity

Relate these findings of neuroscience to the classroom you are observing. What kinds of connections are being made between the real life of students outside the classroom and the subject matter being presented? Are narratives or stories used to enhance the students' contextual understandings of the material? In what ways does the teacher relate new learning to previous learning, thus building on preexisting neural networks? How much choice do students have in determining their studies? Are students allowed to design their own methods of presentation and evaluation?

Reflective Narrative

An important factor that influences the readiness of the human brain for learning is related to tension and stress. Stressful environments initiate "fight or flight" responses in the brain stem and inhibit the firing of neurons in the cerebrum. Knowing this, what can teachers do to reduce the tension in a classroom? Are classrooms inherently stressful for some students? How can teachers present a challenging curriculum without creating a stressful environment?

Related Readings

Cain, R., & Geoffrey, C. (1991). *Making connections: Teaching and the human brain*. Alexandria, VA: Association for Supervision of Curriculum Development.

Goleman, D. (1995). *Emotional intelligence*. New York: Bantam.

Laughlin, C. D., McMannus, J., & D'Aquilli, G. G. (1990). *Brain, symbol, & experience: Toward a neurophenomenology of human consciousness*. Boston: New Science Library.

Liston, D. D. (2001). *Joy as a metaphor of convergence: A phenomenological and aesthetic investigation of social and educational change*. Cresskill, NJ: Hampton.

Sylwester, R. (1995). *A celebration of neurons: An educator's guide to the human brain*. Alexandria, VA: Association for Supervision and Curriculum Development.

CLASSROOM DIALOGUE 1: FREQUENCY[8]

Background

Dialogic interaction is one of the most intricate and complex aspects of classroom teaching. Ensuring that all students have (at the very least) opportunities to participate is an egalitarian goal that is difficult to achieve. However, partialities begin to emerge, as certain students seem to be more adept at dealing with certain questions and problems. When we know which individuals are more likely to answer correctly (or at least answer), they become the anchors of our discussions. If all else fails and the exercise is grinding to a halt, we know we can look to those individuals to "bail us out" and get the discussion moving.

Activity

Observe a classroom where formal discussions are taking place between the teacher and either the entire group or a portion of the class. Doing this exercise in three different sites (elementary, middle/junior high, and high school) would bring an additional dimension to the activity. In the space provided on the data sheet in Fig. 3.3, record your observations of the dialogue between the teacher and the class.

First, construct a matrix of the students using identifiers of sex and broad ethnic groupings (e.g., BF = Black female, AM = Asian male, EF = European female, HM = Hispanic male, etc.).

Then use a simple tally system to record the number of interactions between individual students and the teacher.

Reflective Narrative

Did any patterns develop? Did the teacher serve as a source of encouragement or as a barrier to future participation? Were there some students who were called on more than others? Did students seem to respond to the patterns that the teacher established? Did students who received consistent attention increase their rates of participation? Did students who were not regularly included withdraw from the discussion?

What might you as a future teacher learn from this exercise? What role might your prejudices play in the manner in which you construct the dialogue within your classroom? What might you do to ensure more equitable treatment and opportunities for all your students?

Move on to Classroom Dialogue 2 to further explore this issue.

Related Readings

American Association of University Women. (1993). *How schools shortchange girls: A study of major findings on girls and education.* Washington, DC: American Association of University Women & National Education Association.

Black, L. (2004). Teacher-pupil talk in whole class discussions and the processes of social positioning within the primary school classroom. *Language and Education, 18,* 347–360.

Westgate, D., & Hughes, M. (1997). Identifying "quality" in classroom talk: An enduring research task. *Language and Education, 11,* 125–139.

Identifier	Frequency	Identifier	Frequency

FIG. 3.3.   Classroom Dialogue 1 (reproduce as needed).

CLASSROOM DIALOGUE 2: CONTENT[9]

Background

In the Classroom Dialogue 1 exercise, the focus was on how frequently students were called on. This exercise looks at the content of classroom interactions. Teacher responses to students can vary widely from praise, through indifference, to condemnation. The following is an investigation into teacher response patterns during classroom discussions.

Activity

Observe a classroom in which formal discussions are taking place between the teacher and either the entire group or a portion of the class. Doing this exercise in three different sites—elementary, middle/junior high, and high school—would bring an additional dimension to the activity. In the space provided on your data sheet from Fig. 3.4, record your observations of the dialogue between the teacher and the class.

First, construct a matrix of the students using identifiers of sex and broad ethnic groupings (e.g., BF = Black female, AM = Asian male, EF = European female, HM = Hispanic male, etc.). Then use the following nomenclature to record the content of the interactions between individual students and the teacher.

A Academic (dialogue pertains to the topic)
R Redirect (dialogue designed to bring students back toward the topic, but not a reprimand)

P Praise and/or Validation (affirmation)
M Classroom Management (reprimand)
For example:

BM	BF	AM	AF	EF	EM	HF	HM
A	M	A	R	M	M	A	M
R	P	P	A	M	A	R	
P	A	A			M	M	M

When you have completed your observations, tally the sheets and look for emerging patterns.

Reflective Narrative

Did the teacher serve as a source of encouragement for all students or as a barrier to participation for some? Were some students called on more than others? Were some students praised more than others? Were some students reprimanded more than others? Did students seem to respond to the patterns that the teacher established? Did students who received consistent praise increase their rates of participation? Did students who were regularly reprimanded withdraw from the cognitive discussion and engage in forms of resistance (including silence)?

What might you as a future teacher learn from this exercise? What role might your prejudices play in the way you construct the dialogue within your classroom? What might you do to ensure more equitable treatment and opportunities for all your students?

Related Readings

Deever, B. (1993). A curriculum for educational justice: The social foundations of education and preservice teachers. *Teacher Education Quarterly, 20*(2), 43–56.

Giroux, H. A. (1988). *Teachers as intellectuals: Toward a critical pedagogy of learning.* Hadley, MA: Bergin & Garvey.

Lappe, F. M., & DuBois, P. M. (1993). Others study democracy—We do it. *Democracy and Education, 7*(3), 9–14.

Roman, L. G. (1993). White is a color/white defensiveness, postmodernism, and anti-racist pedagogy. In C. McCarthy & W. Crichelow (Eds.), *Race, identity, and representation in education.* New York: Routledge.

Thompson, B., & Disch, E. (1992). Feminist, anti-racist, anti-oppression teaching: Two White women's experience. *Radical Teacher, 41,* 4–10.

(A) Academic (R) Redirect (P) Praise and/or Validation (M) Classroom Management

FIG. 3.4.   Classroom Dialogue 2 worksheet (reproduce as needed).

CLASSROOM CHARACTERISTICS AND CLIMATE

Background

The purpose of this activity is to record and analyze the characteristics and overall climate of one or more classrooms. Five headings for characteristics have been adapted from the work of Fischer and Fischer.[10]

Task Oriented.   This is the classroom in which prescribed lessons are studied by all students using the same set of resources. Each student works to meet strict preestablished goals that have been described explicitly before the lessons begin. Work time is rigidly controlled.

Cooperative.   This is the classroom in which the teacher has given some control to the students regarding resources, working conditions, timetables, and the like. Although the teacher still retains control over the parameters of the lessons, he or she acts more as a facilitator.

Student Centered.   This is the classroom in which the interests and curiosities of the students guide the direction of their inquiries. In this setting, the subject content is secondary to student interests. The teacher's responsibilities are to support these inquiries along a very broad avenue without becoming directive.

Subject Centered.   This is the classroom in which the content drives all considerations of planning and organization. The student is excluded from consideration. In this setting, the goal is to cover the material as scheduled regardless of student interest or learning.

Learning Centered.   This is the classroom in which a balance is struck between student-centered and subject-centered learning. In this setting, the teacher attempts to honor a commitment both to the individual needs, experiences, and interests of the students and to the subject matter content.

There are two headings under climate that have also been adopted from Fischer and Fischer.[11]

Emotionally Involved.   This is the classroom in which the teacher is personally involved with the learning process as an active participant exhibiting zeal and energy. The result is usually a mix of high emotion and intense personal student involvement. These classrooms may sometimes appear chaotic at first glance.

Emotionally Detached.   This is the classroom in which the teacher sets a tone of dispassionate rationality. Students are challenged through a more orderly process of detached inquiry. The emotional tenor is this setting is subdued but may still exist as a kind of unacknowledged undercurrent that emerges from time to time. This undercurrent is quickly subsumed, however, to dispassionate rationality. The learning that takes place in this setting may be no more or less significant than that which occurs in the emotionally involved classroom.

Activity

After observing two or more classes, think back to the general feelings you perceived in each classroom. On the Characteristics and Climate worksheet from Fig. 3.5, you are asked to indicate the degree to which these teachers created particular learning climates and to assess the characteristics of their classrooms. After observing two or more classes, fill a worksheet out for each of the classrooms and/or teachers you observed. Now compare your results to see if any patterns emerge.

Reflective Narrative

Relate your observations on the classroom characteristics and climate with the goals of democratic participation. Were some classrooms more democratic than others? Did these classrooms exhibit particular characteristics and climates as opposed to those that were more autocratic? Which classrooms seemed more effective in meeting the needs of all the students regardless of their abilities? Which classroom did you prefer? What might that indicate about your preferences as a teacher?

Related Readings

Battistich, V., Solomon, D., & Delucchim, K. (1993). Interaction processes and student outcomes in cooperative learning groups. *Elementary School Journal, 94*(1), 19–32.

Keefe, J. W. (1987). *Learning style theory and practice.* Reston, VA: National Association of Secondary School Principals.

Pierce, C. (1994). Importance of classroom climate for at-risk learners. *Journal of Educational Research, 88,* 37–42.

Vandersijde, P. C., & Tomie, W. (1992). The influence of a teacher training program on student perception of classroom climate. *Journal of Education for Teaching, 18,* 287–295.

Wade, R. C. (1994). Teacher education students views of class discussion: Implications for fostering critical reflection. *Teaching and Teacher Education, 10,* 231–243.

Classroom Characteristics

Indicate where along this continuum you believe the first classroom to be.

Task Oriented _____|_____|_____ Cooperative

Indicate where along this continuum you believe the second classroom to be.

Task Oriented _____|_____|_____ Cooperative

Circle what you believe to be the primary focus of the first classroom.

Student Centered   **Learning Centered**   **Subject Centered**

Circle what you believe to be the primary focus of the second classroom.

Student Centered   **Learning Centered**   **Subject Centered**

Indicate where you believe the first teacher falls on this continuum.

Emotionally Involved _____|_____|_____ **Emotionally Detatched**

Indicate where you believe the second teacher falls on this continuum.

Emotionally Involved _____|_____|_____ **Emotionally Detatched**

FIG. 3.5.   Classroom Characteristics and Climate worksheet (reproduce as needed).

SHADOWING A STUDENT[12]

Background

Many times in teacher training programs we neglect the significant portion of time students are at school but not directly engaged with teachers. What happens in the hallways, on the playground, in the cafeteria, and in those classroom interspaces when the attention of the teacher is directed at other individuals? This exercise is designed to investigate the real life of a student for 1 day. You are trying to understand the world of schooling as seen through the eyes of one student.

Activity

This exercise will be conducted in three phases: the preparation, the observation, and the follow up.

Phase 1: Preparation. In this phase, you will choose a student to shadow for one school day. This activity of course requires you to block out one entire school day. Make sure you are at the school at least 20 min before the arrival of the students, and make sure you have made arrangements for the follow-up interview to be conducted with the student at the end of the observation day. Have someone introduce you to the student so he or she is aware that you will be his or her "shadow" that day. Check your institution's requirements regarding the use of human beings as research participants. Make sure you

follow all the regulations of both your institution and the host school system.

Phase 2: Observation. In this phase, your responsibility is to keep up with the student through the entire school day. Do not follow the student into areas where privacy is a matter of course such as conferences with faculty and/or administrators, the restroom, the infirmary, locker rooms, and the like. Using the observation form from Fig. 3.6, record the activities of the student in approximately 5-min intervals. Record the time, the observed behavior(s), and your understandings of what is occurring (e.g., the student seems bored, excited, etc.). For example:

Time	Observed behavior(s)	Interpretation
9:05	Working in teams with computer.	Seems more interested in *partner* than the task at hand!

Phase 3: Follow-up. This phase is to be conducted with the student at or near the end of the school day depending on both your schedules. During this time, you should ask questions and record his or her responses. Do not be confrontational or argumentative about anything you observed during the day. Your job is to observe, record, and understand the school as seen through the student's eyes—not to judge. You should certainly ask follow-up questions as the

student responds to the primary questions but only for research purposes and not as a form of adjudication or censure.

Reflective Narrative

How does this student appear to understand the school and what is going on? Is this different from what the teachers believe and what you believed from your previous observations? What implications might we draw about how classroom realities are constructed differently by different individuals? What are the implications for your future work as a teacher?

Related Readings

Ellis, J. (1994). Narrative inquiry with children: A generative form of preservice teacher research. *Qualitative Studies in Education, 7*(4), 75–88.

Jardine, D. W. (1989). There are children all around us. *Journal of Educational Thought, 22,* 184–193

Van Manen, M. (1990). *Researching the lived experience: Human sciences for an action sensitive pedagogy*. London, Ontario, Canada: The State University of New York.

Time	Observed Behavior(s)	Interpretation

FIG. 3.6.   Shadowing a Student data form (reproduce as needed).

STUDENT RESISTANCE

Background

For years, many researchers and teachers have worked from the assumption that students were simply passive receptors of knowledge. Because of that, any student behavior not within these parameters of passivity were deemed to be "deviant," and the student was dealt with accordingly. We now know that students are not passive but rather active players in the education process. This means that students have choices as to the nature of their participation running from compliance to resistance.

Resistance can take many forms, both active and passive. Openly subverting the teacher's plans, refusing to follow directions, interrupting, and talking out of turn are all examples of active resistance. Passive resistance is much more subtle but just as effective. Failing to answer, letting the attention wander, sleeping, and day dreaming are all examples of passive resistance.

Activity

Dedicate a portion of your observation time to the issue of student resistance. Watch the students who are not behaving within the norms of classroom rules. What are they doing? Be specific. Are these active or passive acts of resistance? Talk to the students to determine why they did what they did. Were they bored? Were they confused? Were they attempting to hide embarrassment or confusion?

Reflective Narrative

Not all behavior issues in a classroom are the result of deviance. One challenging question that should arise from this exercise concerns the difficulty of determining which acts are resistance and which are simply behavioral issues. Not all misbehavior or passivity are resistance acts. Conversely, not all misbehavior and passivity are socially deviant. How can you tell the difference? Why is it important to know?

Related Readings

Fine, M. (1986). Why urban adolescents drop into and out of public high school. *Teachers College Record, 87,* 393–410.

Gotfrit, L. (1988). Women dancing back: Disruption and the politics of pleasure. *Journal of Education, 170*(3), 122–141.

Pace, B. (2003). Resistance and response: Deconstructing community standards in a literature class. *Journal of Adolescent & Adult Literacy, 46,* 408–412.

Willis, P. (1984). *Learning to labour: How working class kids get working class jobs.* Merrymount, England: Saxon House.

STUDENT RIDICULE AND HARASSMENT

Background

Ever since I can remember, I have been overweight. However, I was used to being teased and had learned to "deal with it." Usually it came from my peers, but this particular day, it came from a different and quite unexpected source. On this particular day, another girl, who was also overweight, had been teased. Everyone except me had called her "jellybelly." And of course she did not like it. She began crying, and I went with her to tell the teacher what had happened. The teacher was very understanding and comforted the girl. As I turned away to go back to the playground, the teacher made a very unexpected comment. She said to me, "Well, Bernice, I don't understand why they didn't pick on you. You are much fatter that she is, and anyone with eyes can see that!" She chuckled, and two of her colleagues who were sitting next to her joined in on the frolic. I was stunned. I just could not believe that a teacher would say something like that to a student. I felt my lip start to quiver, and before I realized it, I blurted out, "You're not so skinny yourself!" With that, she jumped up and took me straight to the principal's office.[13]

As we can witness in the preceding excerpt from the writing of a preservice teacher discussing her significant past school experiences, certain aspects of school life effect some students more than others. Ridicule and harassment are two of these aspects. As we move toward adulthood, this aspect of school life fades in our memory. We have learned how to address more directly most of the confrontational issues that face us in daily life. However, when we were children and adolescents, these strategies were still forming, and the issues of ridicule and harassment loomed large in our daily lives.

Activity

Position yourself in a central location where students congregate between classes or during breaks. This might be a hallway, the cafeteria area, or a playground. Observe the student behaviors and the exchanges that occur. Pay particular attention to comments and actions that are intended to demean and harass. Note the actions and the individuals or groups at whom these actions are targeted.

Reflective Narrative

Who was doing the harassing? Were there patterns to their predations? Who were the targets? How did they react? Did they resist? Did they flee? Can you construct an explanation for these actions? What seemed to be the basis for the intolerance you observed? Was it racial, socioeconomic, gender based, physical, cultural, or something else?

What is your responsibility as a future teacher both legally and ethically to student ridicule and harassment? What did you do? How did this experience make you feel? Did you address any of these issues in the Significant Past School Experiences exercise?

Related Readings

Campbell, W. (2000). Techniques for dealing with student harassment at the high school level. *American Secondary Education, 29*(1), 34–37.

American Association of University Women. (1993). *Hostile hallways: The AAUW survey on sexual harassment in America's schools.* Washington, DC: American Association of University Women and National Education Association.

Grube, B., & Lens, V. (2003). Student-to-student harassment: The impact of *Davis v. Monroe. Children & Schools, 25,* 173–185.

NOTES

[1]Jackson, P. W. (1968). *Life in classrooms.* Chicago: University of Chicago Press.

[2]Martin, J. R. (1976). What do we do with a hidden curriculum when we find one? *Curriculum Inquiry, 6,* 57–74.

[3]Altbach, P. G., Kelly, G. P., Petrie, H. G., & Weis, L. (Eds.). (1991). *Textbooks in American society: Politics, policy, and pedagogy.* Albany: State University of New York Press.

[4]Shannon, P. (1992). Commercial reading materials, a technological ideology, and the deskilling of teachers. In P. Shannon (Ed.), *Becoming political* (pp. 182–207). Portsmouth, NH: Heinemann, p. 196.

[5]Adapted from Page, F. (1994). *Guidelines for student teaching.* Georgia Southern University, Statesboro, GA.

[6]Hart, L. (1983). *Human brain and human learning* (p. 10). New York: Longman.

[7]Laughlin, C. D., McMannus, J., & D'Aquilli, G. G. (1990). *Brain, symbol, & experience: Toward a neurophenomenology of human consciousness.* Boston: New Science Library.

[8]Adapted from an exercise developed by Jane Page, Fred Page, and Donald Hawk (1977), Georgia Southern University, Statesboro, GA.

[9]*Ibid.*

[10]Fischer, B. B., & Fischer, L. (1979, January). Styles in teaching and learning. *Educational Leadership, 36,* 251.

[11]Fischer & Fischer. *Ibid.*

[12]Adapted from an exercise developed by Professor Ronnie Shepherd, Department of Middle Grades and Secondary Education, Georgia Southern University, Statesboro, GA.

[13]Anonymous. (1995). *Reflection paper 1.* Unpublished manuscript, Georgia Southern University, Statesboro, GA.

Section 4

The School as an Ecosystem

INTRODUCTION

An important activity for beginning teacher educators is to reflect on the notions of elite power and control and on democratic participation and decision making as they relate to the local, state, and national levels in our educational bureaucracy. Strong differences within the educational community exist about where certain educational decisions should reside and who should participate in their resolution. This issue has become more complex and complicated in recent years, as the United States has become part of the larger global community and geopolitical world system.

Some educators, for example, are convinced that a greater centralization of power and a more authoritarian state is absolutely essential in the United States to solve successfully the massive social, economic, and ecological problems that confront the nation. Others have a different response to the social crises that confront us. These educators are convinced that the increasing centralization of power is a major contributing cause of the crises, not the cure. As such, they believe that the gradual transfer of power, authority, and control of resources away from neighborhoods, towns, and local schools has undermined our ability, willingness, and initiative to participate in the development of more truly creative and authentic community-based solutions to the problems that confront us. As a preservice teacher educator, it is essential that you grapple with some of the specific dimensions of this complex issue as you pursue your own search for more democratic, participatory, and collaborative models of classroom and school leadership.

In conceptualizing an approach to this section, we decided that exploring metaphors of schooling would be an interesting way to illuminate some competing assumptions, values, norms, control mechanisms, power relationships, and informal communication networks that underlie the organizational culture of American public schooling. Specifically, the images of the school as a factory or machine and as a living ecological web or community network are employed to help you envision and clarify the potential dangers, the hidden assumptions, and the untapped resources that reside in our ideas about schooling in a democratic society. In this section, we have sought to develop a series of reflective exercises that will enable you to investigate some of the basic assumptions about your own host school's organizational structures and cultures. This is so that you might examine them critically and perhaps offer some strategies for creating individually liberating and socially empowering school environments. First, we preview the topics of our study.

Metaphorical Images of Schooling

- Metaphors of Classroom Praxis
- Images in the Classroom

Metaphors help shape the way we view the world and enable us to envision more clearly new ways of understanding ourselves, especially during times of rapid social change. The educational literature is rich in metaphors to describe the nature and functioning of the American public school system. They assist us in our efforts to think about, understand, and describe the ambiguities and complexities of school life. Whether helping us conceive of ourselves as part of a larger interconnected ecological web of human existence or merely as parts of a mechanistic machine designed to serve the interests of an elite few, metaphors can profoundly influence the ways that we choose to participate in the educational process.

Metaphors about schooling have, of course, changed along with our evolving perspectives on our relationship to the world around us. A wide variety of metaphors are available in today's educational literature. In everyday educational discourse and literature, schools are frequently pictured as prisons, factories, shopping malls, families, or gardens. Some like to think of schools as ticking clocks or well-oiled machines that never miss a beat. Others conceptualize schools as high-tech spaceships designed to launch the participants into the new age of high technology. In many of these metaphors, dramatic contradictions and tensions reflect the competing visions and priorities that different social groups have for the public school system.

Two metaphoric images often used in the analysis of organizational life portray the school as a factory or machine and as a living web or community network. These images enable us to envision ways that actions taken by school organizations affect the habitats, cultures, and ecosystems (for better or worse) in which the schools reside. The image of the community network conveys a vision of each school as a dynamic element in the interconnected web of the local geocultural ecological systems. In sharp contrast, a factory carries the impression of a dehumanizing machine that demands conformity, routine, and standardization. Although these metaphoric images are useful for contextualizing oneself in the modern world and in helping one to understand better the kind of tensions and possibilities within organizational life (including that of the U.S. public school system), they tend to represent the ideological opposites of the educational system. Most school organizational structures and cultures rest somewhere between these metaphorical opposites. The preservice teacher can learn, therefore, a great deal about the nature of education and schooling in today's society by exploring these competing metaphorical images.

The metaphor of the factory/machine has become a popular and powerful tool for understanding the nature and functioning of the public school system. Early in the 20th century, Bobbitt[1] argued that "education is a shaping process as much as the manufacture of steel rails" and urged his fellow educators to apply the principles of scientific management to every aspect of school administration and operation. In the same way, the sociologist Ross[2] suggested that to educate was "to collect little plastic lumps of human dough from private households and shape them on the social kneading board." School administrators often are compared to factory managers, concerned only with the bottom line: efficiency, productivity, product, work pace, and the like. Perhaps the most important aspect of this metaphor is that it speaks to the technical operational nature of our human relationships and renders all natural aspects of life as largely instrumental: Humans, the environment, animals, and industry all are subsumed under the concept of the machine.

This technological vision of organizations was rapidly applied to education. Today, educators argue that schools are formal organizations and as such, are like giant computers with inputs and outputs, feedback loops, scientifically generated curriculum, and standardized evaluation systems. Administrators are seen as responsible for keeping the gears running smoothly, ensuring the efficient operation of daily work routines and the general maintenance of the school facilities. They are empowered to supervise, punish, evaluate, and reward so as to maintain operational efficiency.

Teachers are forced into a dependency relationship with school administrators and the rest of the educational hierarchy. They work under conditions largely beyond their control, implementing national and state-mandated standards in which they have little or no input. Underlying such top-down mechanistic approaches to educational decision making are unstated beliefs about the desirability of having large-scale, federal- and state-level educational bureaucracies set nationwide standardized systems of evaluation. Heilbroner,[3] for example, argued, "I not only predict but I prescribe a centralization of power as the only means by which our threatened and dangerous civilization can make way for its successor."

The image of the school as an ecological web is grounded in the image of caring, sharing, and of mutual coexistence. Because we are all connected, we all should act cooperatively to maintain and preserve our collective work environments. Perhaps de Chardin[4] expressed it best when he wrote the following:

> The farther and more deeply we penetrate into matter, by means of increasingly powerful methods, the more we are confounded by the interdependence of its parts. Each element of the cosmos is positively woven from all the others.... It is impossible to cut into this network, to isolate a portion without it becoming frayed and unraveled at all its edges. All around us, as far as the eye can see, the universe holds together, and only one way of considering it is really possible, that is, to take it as a whole, in one piece.[4]

From this perspective, one's living body is seen as part of a complex but fragile system of interdependent relationships that depends on cooperation, connectedness, and community for its very existence. Here, we see ourselves and others as part of a collective whole, an organic "Gaia," a universal classroom, a part of an interconnected global web of alliances and obligations. At its core, then, the living body web metaphor resonates with a concern for the delicacy of the strands that connect us and provide us with sustenance: It dramatically captures the theme that we affect everything and everything affects us.

This metaphor of the school as a living body/community web is one that we often use more commonly in rhetorical writings about educa-

tion. In such formulations, the school often is described as a family, home, team, or womb. The principal is described as a parent, nurturer, friend, sibling, or coach. In such school organizational cultures, colleagues have a great concern for one another as well as a commitment to students that goes above and beyond the call of duty. Not unlike that of biological families, an extensive network exists of informal food, entertainment, sports, and holiday rituals (i.e., birthday celebrations, betting pools, informal communication networks, friendly jokes, etc.) that binds the faculty and staff to one another and provides multiple avenues for socializing and bonding. In such schools, teachers view each other as competent professionals who may not always agree with one another but who must respect one another and have each other's best interest at heart. Parents are welcomed guests and volunteers. Teachers and students share tasks and conegotiate learning options in education cultures that are collegial, respectful, and collaborative. Participants accept the legitimacy and authority of the organization because they are an integral part of the decision-making process.

These metaphorical oppositions can be more closely examined to illustrate both the pitfalls and possibilities that exist in our educational settings today. They also have the ability to help us to understand some of our own changing attitudes toward education and analyze some of the existing tensions in public school environments. We invite you to do just this in the exercise developed for this section.

Studying About Your Host School's Power Structures

- Student Governance
- Faculty and Staff Governance
- Role of the Local School Board
- Process of Educational Decision Making

Contemporary school reform literature is replete with metaphors, images, and words that convey democratic principles and values. Central to any contemporary discourse or textual elaboration of the current school reform initiatives are words such as community, community control, decentralization, participation, empowerment, parental involvement, student decision making, teacher control, local control, site-based management, the self-managed school, collaborative decision making, self-determining school systems, and parental choice. These words lead one to believe that educational structures and processes have indeed begun to move toward more locally based and participatory democratic forms. Is it true that the metaphor of the school as a factory has begun to be replaced by that of the school as an ecological web?

Many educational theorists and school practitioners have pointed out, however, that the hoped for shift in the nature of educational decision making from the older models of control-oriented, top-down management to more democratic modes of local site-based management has not occurred.[5] These same educational theorists have pointed out that the national educational "empowerment" discourse of the 1990s only functions to obscure and mask the recentralization of educational decision making in a professional elite that is occurring throughout the educational bureaucracy. Reflecting on these differing perspectives, Smyth[6] asked some troubling questions concerning the precise nature of these latest school reform strategies:

> The paradox is that at precisely the same time we are experiencing a hardening of the educational arteries through moves to make schooling more "rigorous," "disciplined," and "scholarly" (all of which are only really possible in circumstances where final decision-making is vested in the hands of an elite decision-making group), we are also being courted by moves that appear to make the schools more "self-determining" and "self-renewing," with teachers who are more "autonomous," "empowered," "collaborative," and "reflective." How do we explain this paradox?[6]

This second group of exercises has been developed to help you think about some of the issues involved in this current educational debate within the context of your own host school. What has been the impact of the latest school restructuring efforts at your school? We invite you to look beyond the rhetoric of the school reform literature today and study the actual changes that have been institutionalized as part of the current school restructuring movement at your school. Ask your colleagues the following questions: Have the new models of site-based management been more emancipatory and liberating for teachers, students, and school administrators? Or has the current school restructuring movement functioned only to allow a system of national standards, curriculum, evaluation, and testing to be adopted within a framework that puts the burden of implementation, funding, and accountability on local school systems? Is this the best model of democratic decision making you can envision? As future educators, it is essential that you begin to develop the kind of critical consciousness and analytic skills that will allow you to investigate these issues in greater depth. These exercises are also designed to encourage you to think about what a more socially, culturally, and politically empowering approach to democratic decision making might resemble.

Exploring School–Community Linkages

- Assessing Family–School Relationships
- Assessing the Parent–Teacher Relationship
- School-to-Work Linkages
- Extracurricular School Activities
- Rebellion, Conformity, and Making Do
- Violent Schools–Safe Schools: Police–Military Linkages
- Consumerism in the Classroom
- Cyberspace and the Virtual Classroom

We hear a lot these days about a "sense of community." More and more of us, we're told, are seeking it. We talk about the African American, Hispanic, and Asian communities; the gay and lesbian community; the New Age community;

the political community; the university community; a community of peers; a community of interests; the local community. But what is this thing called community? Why do we seek it? How do we know when we find it?[7]

What is a democratic community? What are the purposes of public schools? Indeed, the very concepts of community and democracy have become obscure and somewhat remote from our everyday lived experiences. We often hear others say that democratic forms of self-government have become increasingly irrelevant in today's high-tech global economy and that we need to generate more realistic, professionally viable, and managed forms of democratic participation. It is clear that we live in an age with multiple perspectives on what constitutes a democratic community and democratic schooling. Some argue that schools should be an arena where special interest groups are allowed to compete within the framework of a free market ideology based on self-interest, competition, and choice.[8] McDaniel[9] and Shea[10] have argued that much of this school reform rhetoric is grounded in military metaphors and images such as: strategic planning, systems analysis, social efficiency, accountability, and disciplinary enforcement. The power of such metaphoric images of schooling is in their ability to define what and who shall be included or excluded from the discussion, decision making, and implementation of educational policy.

By contrast, educators such as Kozol,[11] Orr,[12] Bowers,[13] Smith,[14] Traina and Darley-Hill,[15] Henderson and Kesson,[16] Esteva and Prakash,[17] and Sobel,[18] among others, have emphasized that the revival of more democratic, participatory forms of public schooling in the United States rests on the simultaneous rebuilding of local communities, small towns, urban wards, and cohesive neighborhood networks that have suffered from decades of neglect. *Bioregionalism* is the name given to these various attempts to rejuvenate regional and local institutions to recreate the kind of rich system of interactive and participatory local networks needed for healthy com-

munity-based schools in the 21st century. Along similar lines, others have argued that the top-down, control-oriented models of democratic management have resulted in the decline of local communities as repositories of commitment, loyalty, and obligation. Only by a revival of such soulful and intimate community structures can authentic local traditions and values flourish and be reinforced, developed, and celebrated. Winters reminded us that "community should be a place where compassion abounds and where individuals are valued for their uniqueness."[19]

We wonder anew: Who should control our schools and how? In the United States, with our multilayered governmental bureaucratic structures, educational decision making is formally distributed and delegated among a variety of professional groups including state and federal judges, the Secretary of Education, appointed presidential advisors, the Congress and state legislatures, mayors and city councils, and civil servant bureaucrats. In addition, a variety of extralegal pressure groups vie for power and control at the federal, state, and local levels of the educational bureaucracy. Such groups include professional groups, teacher unions, philanthropic foundations, corporate leaders, organized special interest groups, think tanks, and lobbyists. The plethora of competing and allied groups makes it imperative that we describe and differentiate between competing models of democratic empowerment and control.[20]

Although drawing analogies between school organizations and factories and picturing school organizations as interconnected community webs helps us reflect on some of the characteristics that define different organizational structures, it does not allow us to experience the innermost essence of school cultures: those taken-for-granted, invisible, and often unconscious aspects of school life. Recent educational writings have identified a number of these elements through which school organizational structures and cultures are preserved, expressed, and conveyed including the history of the school, symbolic myths and stories, values and beliefs, behavioral norms, rites and rituals, and heroes and heroines. These cultural forms and the hidden network of informal connections and relationships will also be a part of your observations and reflections in this section.

Your exploration of these competing metaphors of schooling will illuminate some of the opposing assumptions, values, norms, control mechanisms, power relationships, and informal communication networks that underlie the organizational cultures in our public schools. The aim of these exercises is not to force you to choose one metaphor over another but rather to show you the ways in which our public schools have become complex, political arenas on which differing social groups seek to realize their individual educational agendas. In the end, you will return, as you began, with the question, What is the nature of a democratic community? What are (and should be) the purposes of democratic schools? How can I as a politically informed teacher work toward further democratizing our public school classrooms?

METAPHORS OF CLASSROOM PRAXIS

Background

Metaphor plays an important part in human thought processes. Although commonly associated with poetry, metaphors increase our understanding in many fields, enabling us to understand one kind of thing in terms of another. In this way, we gain a greater understanding of an unfamiliar or complex object or idea in terms of a more familiar or less complex object or idea. Additionally, metaphors provide a bridge of understanding by establishing a common connection between two people experiencing difficulty grasping one another's perspectives.

For example, a common metaphor useful for the fieldwork experience portrays the classroom as a mirror of the larger society. Our familiarity with the relatively simple mirror concept can be used to enhance our understanding of the more complex concept of public schools. By exploring this metaphor, we can reflect on educational issues from a new perspective and generate new insights on possible connections between social structures and classroom praxis.[21]

Activity

In the following list are metaphors commonly used in describing the American public school system today: School is like a …

war

drugstore

factory

prison

shopping mall

stream

babysitting service

health club

family

journey

garden

smorgasbord

spaceship

living body

circus

cemetery

ant colony

church/religious services

spider web

battlefield

hospital ward

TV game show

dog kennel

baseball game

Select one metaphor from the preceding list or create one of your own for further exploration. Consider first the classroom environment that you are observing. How is the metaphor you selected represented? You may want to start by making a list of terms from education that correspond to the metaphor you have selected. For example, if you selected "war," who is the enemy? What are the weapons? Who is the supply sergeant, the general, the deserters, the casualties? How do classroom materials relate to the metaphor?

Write a brief analysis of your insights. What is the significance of the observations you made? What can you determine about the extent to which this metaphor represents an ideal to which we can aspire or a danger that we should attempt to avoid? Consider also the implications of this metaphor for teachers, students, administrators, and parents. What kind of teacher–student relationships does the metaphor encourage? What role does the metaphor suggest for parents? What does this metaphor indicate about the curriculum? Are certain subjects highlighted by the use of this metaphor? Are other subjects difficult to imagine within this context?

Reflective Narrative

You may want to select a second metaphor to explore for comparison or to compare with those chosen by your classmates. How does this second metaphor change the way you think about schools? Can you think of other metaphors that may relate to education? How do these other perspectives affect your understanding of the activities of schooling? Does any single metaphor account for every aspect and dimension of education? What metaphor do you think is best and why? In what ways might these metaphors influence our experiences (and behaviors) in schools?

Related Readings

Clarken, R. H. (1997, March). *Five metaphors for educators*. Paper presented at the annual meeting of the American Education Research Association, Chicago, IL.

Davidson, D. (1978). What metaphors mean. *Critical Inquiry, 5,* 31–47.

Giroux, H. A. (1981). *Ideology, culture, and the process of schooling.* London: Falmer.

Lakoff, G., & Johnson, M. (1980). *Metaphors we live by.* Chicago: University of Chicago Press. (See especially "Concepts We Live By" [pp. 3–6] and "Metaphor and Cultural Coherence" [pp. 22–24].)

Morgan, G. (1986). *Images of organization.* Beverly Hills, CA: Sage.

Rehm, M. (1994). Critical pedagogy and vocational education: A search for new metaphors. In R. D. Lakes (Ed.), *Critical education and work: Multidisciplinary approaches* (pp. 143–160). Norwood, NJ: Ablex.

Tobin, K. (April, 1990). Metaphors in the construction of teacher knowledge. Paper presented at the annual meeting of the American Research Association, Boston, MA.

Wilson, B. G. (1995). Metaphors for instruction: Why we talk about learning environments. *Educational Technology, 35*(5), 25–30.

IMAGES IN THE CLASSROOM

Background

We are constantly surrounded by images of all kinds. One of the frequently overlooked aspects of the classroom environment is the images. We are constantly surrounded by images of all kinds. In today's schools, almost every classroom has a television set and computers that relay images to students and teachers. Yet other images are in the classroom: bulletin boards with photographs, illustrations, drawings, and announcements. Although we often tune out these images, they still affect our behaviors and attitudes and reveal much about the values embedded in the daily practice of schooling.

Activity

Take inventory of the images you see in the classroom. What is being represented? Are films, videos, or television programs part of the curriculum? What commercials or advertisements are associated with these programs?

What about the bulletin boards in the classroom? Are these announcement centers or decorations? Are they used in conjunction with the curriculum materials and texts? Do they support formal learning? Are the images stale or are they replaced frequently? Notice also the images in the textbooks. How is the artwork presented in the texts and on the covers? What images are found within the texts? Who is represented? What are they doing? Note differences in gender, race or ethnicity, and social class. How are various social groups depicted? After making a thorough accounting of the images in the classroom, gather your data and write up your analysis.

Reflective Narrative

Do the images in the classroom present a coherent and carefully planned message? Are they consistent and complementary in their presentations, or are they contradictory and confusing? How are the images in the classroom different from images in religious settings, shopping malls, homes, restaurants, and highways?

What kinds of images did you still overlook in your first observation? Did you find images on notebooks, pens, and pencils? Did you note clothes of students and teachers that advertise products or ideas? Did you find any desks, chairs, or other objects in the room with images carved on them? Make another inspection of the room, and determine what you may have left out the first time. Why were these images overlooked during your first inspection?

Related Readings

Douglas, S. (1994). *Where the girls are: Growing up female with the mass media*. New York: Times Books.

Ellsworth, E., & Whatley, M. H. (Eds.). (1990). *The ideology of images in educational media: Hidden curriculums in the classroom*. New York: Teachers College Press.

McLaren, P. (1986). *Schooling as ritual performance: Towards a political economy of educational symbols and gestures*. London: Routledge & Kegan Paul.

Rosen, E. Y., Quesada, A. P., & Summers, S. L. (1998). *Changing the world through media education.* Golden, CA: Fulcrum.

Spring, J. (1994). *Images of American life: A history of ideological management in schools, movies, radio, and television.* Albany: State University of New York Press.

Video Recordings

Riggs, M. J. (1987). *Ethnic notions.* California News Reel.

Kilbroun, J. (1987). *Still killing us softly: Advertising images of women.* Cambridge, MA: Cambridge Documentary films.

STUDENT GOVERNANCE AND DECISION MAKING

Background

Student governance and decision making are perhaps the most controversial and least understood components in the new site-based management models of school restructuring. Students are not generally viewed as having the cognitive, psychological, moral, or emotional maturity needed to make reasonable and responsible choices concerning their own educational programs, learning environments, and work pace. Students usually are viewed as consumers or products of the educational process; teachers are viewed as the proper classroom authorities in all matters related to curriculum, pedagogy, rules, and discipline. Most school curricula are set, and instruction is centered on the mastery of a state-mandated set of grade-specific standards. Nationally standardized tests control and shape an increasing amount of the students' in-class learning experiences and required texts. Not unexpectedly, this sort of top-down classroom "colonization" of students has resulted in myriad forms of student subservience, acquiescence, passivity, retreat, disruption, and revolt.[22]

As school systems struggle to revise and transform older administrative structures based on top-down management systems designed to ensure compliance, order, predictability, and social control, new concepts of school leadership and empowerment have been adopted by school administrators, teachers, and students. The school in which you presently reside most likely contains an odd combination of both organizational models. Student empowerment suggests that students are a central part of the educational process and should be encouraged to take increasing responsibility for their educational work. In this sense, teachers and students share tasks and co-negotiate learning options in educational cultures that are collegial, respectful, and collaborative. The goal of student empowerment is to take a student from dependency to independence.[23]

Activity

This exercise is designed to position you as an investigator into the nature and degree of student power and participation in the decision-making structures of the larger school organization.

1. Obtain and examine a copy of the student handbook at your host school. What topics are addressed? What do most of the standing regulations seem to address: behavior? clothing? conformity? allegiance to the organization?

2. Attend some of the regularly scheduled meetings of the student government. Discover how student government is organized at your school and what specific responsibilities are delegated to it. What is the scope and nature of the decision-making powers assigned to the student government? Do most of the "decisions" appear to be preordained? What issues appear to be out of bounds? For example, to what extent is student government involved in course selection and development, teacher evaluation, school management and budget decisions, scheduling

decisions, luncheon menus, and disciplinary procedures? Is student government largely relegated to decisions concerning bulletin boards, prom queen, fund raisers, weekend dance or events arrangements, or class trip planning? Do you feel a sense of real empowerment in this group? If so, why? To what do you attribute this?

Reflective Narrative

Most student organizations have very limited powers and regularly address only issues of little relevance to the larger school and district-wide educational bureaucracies. Interview some of the student leaders and members of the various student cliques concerning their perceptions of the school power structures. Through informal conversations with these various student subcultures, attempt to develop a slang classificatory system for all terms used to identify student groups within the school (i.e., the *nerds*, the *jocks*, the *social climbers*, the *preppies*, the *druggies*, etc.). Ask them some of the following questions: Who seems to control the dominant culture of the student organizations in terms of defining the acceptable boundaries of behavior? Which student subgroups are most actively involved in student government and why? How is membership determined? Do the student leaders seem to represent all the students or just a particular subculture of the students? Or are they merely those most willing to implement mandates from the administrative staff?

Related Readings

Apple, M., & Beane, J. A. (1995). *Democratic schools.* Alexandria, VA: Association for Supervision and Curriculum Development.

Eckert, P. (1989). *Jocks and burnouts: Social categories and identity in the high school.* New York: Teachers College Press.

Greenberg, D. (1991). *Free at last: The Sudbury Valley School.* Farmingham, MA: Sudbury Valley School Press.

Smith, G. A. (1993). *Public schools that work.* New York: Routledge & Kegan Paul.

Wood, G. (1992). *Schools that work.* New York: Dutton.

FACULTY AND STAFF GOVERNANCE

Background

Schools are both organizations and communities. They contain within them sophisticated networks (formal and informal) of adult subcultures (e.g., the administrators, teachers, coaches, maintenance staff, secretaries, paraprofessionals, tenured and nontenured faculty, men and women, etc.) as well as youth subcultures. Although each of these subcultures has its own informal boundaries, rituals, and rules, they all must exist and function within the boundaries and regulations of the larger school organizational structure, interacting with one another and the larger society. This larger school culture is considered the dominant culture, whereas the others are regarded as subcultures. School rules and regulations are often ways of maintaining the dominant culture of the organization against the dynamic pressures from subcultural groups for greater participation. School rules also work to maintain a certain set of power relationships between various groups in the school. The manner in which governance (decision making) occurs within the organization is clearly linked to these interests of power.[24]

Subcultural groups both control and are controlled by the school organizations in which they serve. In a sense, there is a continual dialogue among subcultural groups themselves and with the administrative elite. This creates a dynamic tension in a school no matter how autocratic, conformist, or participatory its basic organizational structure. In most American public schools, these subcultural relationships are perceived as threats to the status quo and impediments to the smooth, top-down administration of the educational bureaucracy. Thus, a dominant organizational culture develops dedicated largely to managing change and maintaining control.[25]

Activity

With the assistance of a trusted member of your school's faculty, examine the manner in which faculty governance is conducted at your host school.[26] How is governance organized? What is its position on a flow chart of the school or the school district? Who serves? How is membership determined? Are the faculty "leaders" chosen merely to be "rubber stamps" of administrative decisions, or is it the other way around with administrators selected because they have a history of supporting teacher empowerment? Who are the department or program chairpersons? What are their roles and responsibilities? Does any one person or any one group have the informal power to control decision making? How did they gain such informal power and influence?

What issues are addressed by these faculty and staff groups? How much real input does the faculty have regarding curricular, personnel, programs, policy, or financial decisions? Is faculty governance merely advisory or does the faculty have any real power of decision making? Observe how and what changes take place at your school. Do the faculty seem more concerned with the meeting their own needs, satisfying administrators, or helping students?

Do the faculty at the school appear to be satisfied or concerned about the decision-making power they have (or do not have) at this school? If they are concerned about their lack of empowerment, does it get expressed through the formal political process or more often through informal acts of defiance and resistance (i.e., leaving when the school bell rings, sitting passively in faculty meetings, etc.)? Are the custodial staff, secretaries, and paraprofessionals ever included in the faculty decision-making bodies? If not, why? How are beginning teachers mentored into these multiple decision-making frameworks? What do the new teachers at your host school believe to be the most difficult and challenging issues discussed at faculty meetings? Do they believe these issues are being adequately addressed and resolved in a timely manner?

In what kind of political activity are the faculty at your host school allowed to participate? Are they allowed to become actively involved in school board elections or hold political office? Are teachers allowed to organize at the school? Have there been any strikes? If so, what were the issues? Talk to the teachers at your school, particularly the union organizers. Do the teachers' organizations influence decision making at the school? How much influence do they exert? What are the issues? Are there union contracts at the school? Review these contracts for their provisions regarding salaries, curriculum structuring, class size, and so forth. Do you see any connections being established between teacher governance structures, increased democratic decision-making formats, and greater community involvement in the school?

Reflective Narrative

How do the faculty and staff governance structures compare with the student governance structures? Whose interests do the faculty governance structures seem to favor: staff's? teachers'? administrators'? parents'? no one's? Are the administrative, faculty, staff, and student governance structures mutually informing and supportive, or do their aims seem to be at odds with one another?

Related Readings

Ayers, W. (1993). *To teach: The journey of a teacher.* New York: Teachers College Press.

Carlson, D. (1992). *Teachers and crisis: Urban school reform and teachers' work culture.* New York: Routledge & Kegan Paul.

Henderson, J. G., & Kesson, K. (Eds.). (1999). *Understanding democratic curriculum leadership.* New York: Teachers College Press.

Martin, R. (2001). *Listening up: Reinventing ourselves as teachers and students.* Portsmouth, NH: Boynton/Cook-Heinemann.

Miller, J. P. (1993). *The holistic teacher.* Toronto, Ontario, Canada: Ontario Institute for Studies in Education.

Shor, I. (1992). *Empowering education: Critical teaching for social change.* Chicago: University of Chicago Press.

Smyth, J. (1991). *Teachers as collaborative learners: Challenging dominant forms of supervision.* Philadelphia: Open University Press.

Snowden, P. E., & Groton, R. A. (2001). *School leadership and administration: Important concepts, case studies, & simulations.* New York: McGraw-Hill Higher Education.

ROLE OF LOCAL SCHOOL BOARDS

Background

The framers of the United States Constitution made no mention of education but left that responsibility instead to the states through the reserved powers' clause. In turn, most states, in their constitution or laws, decided that the operational governance functions for schools should reside in local school boards. In the 19th century, governance was lodged in school boards largely responsive to local community cultures and traditions. However, by the 1890s, rapid immigration, urbanization, industrialization, and business consolidations brought many changes to American society. As part of the progressive municipal reform movement, educational governance systems were centralized, and 120,000 local school boards were consolidated into what are now only 14,256. Leadership shifted to a new professional middle-class group trained in the theories of scientific management, and large statewide educational bureaucracies grew at exponential rates. Today, almost one half of our public school population is enrolled in only 1% of our school districts. As a result, many concede that we have now constructed massive educational bureaucracies that enable national and state control over almost every aspect of local schooling in the United States.[27]

The National School Boards Association[28] issued a major report in 2002 that sought to illuminate the nature of school boards in the United States and the challenges they face. The most striking conclusion from their findings is that large-district boards are fundamentally different from their smaller, more plentiful, counterparts. In large districts (defined as those with 25,000 or more students), school boards functioned in a decidedly more political fashion with greater participation from more ideologically oriented interest groups and school board candidates. On the other hand, the survey found that school boards in small districts tended to be relatively apolitical bodies that attracted little attention or political controversy. In addition, the survey found distinct differences in the school policy concerns that school board members in small versus larger school districts rate as being most pressing in their individual school districts.

Not surprisingly, however, this same survey found that the profiles of school board members themselves were strikingly similar. School boards are less racially diverse than the nation as a whole; overall, school board members identify themselves as 85% White. School board members are about 61% male and 39% female. In addition, the vast majority of school superintendents is still disproportionately White and male (i.e., about 85%). Board members typically have an annual income that exceeds the national average; most report incomes of $75,000 or more. Board members fall predominantly into the upper middle class, a pattern that holds across districts of all sizes. Board members as a group are significantly more educated than the broader American public; almost all board members (i.e., 96%) are parents, and about half of them have children currently in school.

Your own school board is likely to reflect many of the same characteristics as revealed by this latest comprehensive survey of American school boards. Your job in this assignment is to begin to think about what kind of reforms you would like to see in how school boards are chosen, how they are structured, what they do, and/or the school policies they focus on in their deliberations. In light of these findings, it seems reasonable to inquire, too, to what extent the varying size, needs, environmental context, and financial resources of individual school districts should determine and shape their discussions of school policies.

Activity

Attend a local school-board meeting. Before or after the meeting, introduce yourself to some of the members of the school board and ask whether you might interview them either in person or by phone at a time and place convenient for them.

After gathering some initial profile data on your school board member, tell your interviewee that you would like to find out more about what school-related issues are of most interest to school-board members. Use the chart from Fig. 4.1 to record the board member's responses. Take the survey yourself; observe the similarities and differences in your responses.

Consider the following questions: Do you think the similarities or differences discovered between any of the individuals surveyed are due to the following factors: gender? social class? education? school knowledge or participation? age? What findings were particularly troubling for you as you reviewed your survey results? On the basis of your findings, do you have any recommendations for your school board? For example, on the basis of your findings, would you suggest a greater representation on your school board from certain social groups? Which ones? Would you recommend some areas in which your local school board could benefit from additional training and informative workshops? Find out if students are allowed to serve on school boards in your state. If so, are they allowed to vote?

Reflective Narrative

Study the responses made by yourself and the school board members to your survey. Then give the same survey to some of the teachers and administrators at your host school. Do you notice any trends in their responses, especially to your questions about the importance of certain educational issues? Write a short response to your survey indicating how and why your own responses seem to be different from or the same as those provided by school board members, administrators, or the teachers at your host school.

Related Readings

Grady, M. L. (1995). Superintendents' and school board members' perceptions of empowerment. In M. Richardson, K. Lane, & J. Flanigan (Eds.), *School empowerment* (pp. 199–212). Lancaster, PA: Technomic Publishing Company.

Hess, F. M. (2002). *School boards at the dawn f the 21st century*. Alexandria, VA: National School Boards Association.

Howell, W. (2005). *Besieged: School boards and the future of American politics*. Washington, DC: Brookings Institution Press.

School-Related Concerns	Little Interest	Some Interest	Great Interest
1. Funding, budget, resource allocation			
2. Collective bargaining, merit pay for teachers			
3. Parental participation, support, interest			
4. Site-based management			
5. Teacher quality, professional development			
6. Inadequate facilities, overcrowding			
7. Curriculum development, enrichment			
8. School tracking, inclusion			
9. Crime, vandalism, school property			
10. State-mandated curriculum reforms			
11. Racial/ethnic tensions and concerns			
12. At-risk/special education programs			
13. Student truancy, apathy, dropout problem			
14. School and district management and leadership			
15. School and business partnerships			
16. School choice, charter schools, home schooling			
17. Implementing national standards, NCLB			
18. Student diversity, equity issues			
19. Upgrading educational technology, computers			
20. Student achievement issues			
21. Alternative certification, licensure for teachers			
22. Board and community engagement opportunities			
23. Teacher shortages, fast-track teacher training programs			
24. School safety and security issues			
25. Accountability and high-stakes testing			
26. Community collaboration and partnerships			
27. School climate and morale issues			

FIG. 4.1.   School Board Members' Concerns and Interests Survey Form[29] (reproduce as needed).

POLITICS OF EDUCATIONAL DECISION MAKING

Background

Before the 1960s, local community participation in educational decision making during the 20th century was limited not only in terms of who participated and how but also in the range of educational issues deemed appropriate for grassroots input.[30] There was a tacit assumption that most educational decisions required technical expertise and therefore should be delegated to educational professionals. Issues relating to governance, budget, personnel, curriculum, and discipline were generally considered outside the realm of local citizenry.

Much of this changed as a result of the community control movement in the 1960s as the old consensus broke down. Newly politicized groups of minorities and women, formerly excluded from the educational decision-making process, demanded to be heard. The idea that schools were essentially technocratically engineered, bureaucratic "machines" best run by the professionals was attacked. Although this community control movement did not produce any dramatic restructuring of political power in the educational bureaucracy, it did broaden the scope of local participation in many aspects of school decision making.

As a result of these early experiments in community control, today many large city school districts have adopted some form of administrative decentralization with varying degrees of community participation. Some school districts have begun experimental community-controlled schools, and thousands of others are adding new parent/citizen advisory committees. A number of Indian tribes have initiated community control experiments in their reservation schools. Generally, it can be concluded that more parents and other nonprofessional community members are participating than ever before in a wide-ranging number and variety of school programs and operations as tutors, volunteers, librarians, lunchroom assistants, hall monitors, classroom paraprofessionals, leaders for extracurricular activities, special resource teachers, and the like.[31]

We are now being inundated with a bewildering array of terms such as *school-based management, site-based management, the self-managing school, the self-renewing school, and school empowerment*. These terms lead us to conclude that the impact of the current reform movements has been to further increase local participation by students, parents, teachers, administrators, and local citizens in all aspects of the local community. Unmasking appearances is the purpose of the following exercise. Ask yourself the following questions about the nature of educational decision making: In what issues do students, parents, teachers, administrators, and/or local citizens participate? In what ways do they participate? What are the consequences of their participation?

Activity

Complete the left side of the chart in Fig. 4.2 by finding out who actually does control the decision making regarding each of the educational issues listed (list as many numbers as apply).

Complete the right side of this same chart. Interview several teachers and administrators at your school about who should control (or have more input into the decision-making process of) each of the educational issues listed. To assist your interviewees, ask them to examine the chart from Fig. 4.3 and tell you who should have more control over each educational issue. Make a list of as many of the numbers as the respondent wishes to use.

Following your survey of teachers and administrators, look around your own classroom and the school classrooms, halls, and meeting rooms. Do you see any explicit messages to the students encouraging their participation in the school decision-making bodies? Are there bulletin boards with up-to-date information on the issues being discussed by students, teachers, administrators, parents, and the local school board? Does the school Web site or bulletin board provide a listing of the current names, addresses, phone numbers, and e-mail addresses of contact persons within each organization? Are there any formal structures, procedures, or networks so that students can easily provide their informal input on these issues? What recommendations might you make to the school administrators on ways to improve the process by which students can be informed and can contribute their ideas to the various decision-making groups in the school? Ask teachers at your school the extent to which their preservice teacher education programs prepared them to participate in school policy debates and processes.

Reflective Narrative

Study the responses to your survey made by the teachers and administrators. Did you notice any trends in their responses? For example, did you find that teachers are almost never formally included in most of the important school-related decision making? Did you find that the teachers desired some form of input on most of these issues? Can you think of some good reasons why the insights, perspectives, and experiences of the classroom teachers might be essential in making good policy decisions on these issues? Can you think of why teachers have been excluded from the political process for so long? Did you find that the teachers desired a greater degree of student input on these issues too? If not, why do you think this is the case? Do you think that students should be included to a greater degree in the formal decision-making bodies of the school?

Related Readings

Giroux, H. (1989). Educational reform and teacher empowerment. In H. Holtz, I. Mareus, J. Dougherty, J. Michaels, & R. Peduzzi (Eds.), *Education and the American dream: Conservatives, liberals, and radicals debate the future of education* (pp. 173–186). Granby, MA: Bergin & Garvey.

Maeroff, G. I. (1988). *The empowerment of teachers: Overcoming the crisis of confidence.* New York: Teachers College Press.

O'Hair, M. J., McLaughlin, H. J., & Reitzug, U. C. (2000). *Foundations of democratic education.* Orlando, FL: Harcourt College Publishers.

Rocha, D. L. S. (2003). *Schools where children matter: Exploring educational alternatives.* Brandon, VT: Foundation for Educational Renewal.

Sernak, K. (1998). *School leadership—Balancing power with caring.* New York: Teachers College Press.

Smith, G. (1994). Preparing teachers to restructure schools. *Journal of Teacher Education, 45,* 18–30.

Zeichner, K. (1991). Contradictions and tensions in the professionalism of teaching. *Teachers College Record, 92,* 363–373.

Does Participate?	School Policy Decisions	Should Participate?
	To assess student performance/achievement?	
	To elect the school principal?	
	To elect local superintendent?	
	To close a school?	
	Formulate school disciplinary policies?	
	School schedule? Classroom schedules?	
	Decide lunchroom menus?	
	Formulate teacher qualification policies?	
	Vote on teacher placement/retention?	
	Choose classroom textbooks?	
	Determine attendance policy?	
	Responsibility for school budget/resource allocation?	
	Determine school dress policy?	
	Determine classroom-level grading policies?	
	Determine whether school is providing equality of educational opportunity?	
	Number/type of courses for graduation?	
	Mainstreaming policies?	
	Corporeal punishment rules?	
	Racial balance of students?	
	Classroom curriculum and methodology review?	
	Teacher Salaries?	
	Professional development opportunities/ workshops?	
	Standardized testing procedures	
	School security issues	
	Tracking/inclusion policies	

FIG 4.2. The politics of educational decision making: Who does or should control? (reproduce as needed).

Local Level Groups	State Level Groups
1. Parents at local level 2. Local boards of education 3. School principal 4. Student council 5. Local education associations (PTA) 6. Teacher council at each school 7. Teachers 8. Local district superintendent 9. Members/citizens of the community 10. Students 11. School staff (e.g., bus drivers, dieticians, health officers, attendance officers) 12. Local police departments 13. Local business groups	27. State legislatures 28. State boards of education 29. State superintendent 30. The governor 31. Governor's ad hoc task forces on education 32. State department of education 33. Urban city majors 34. Urban city councils
National Level Groups	**Extra-Legal/Pressure Groups**
14. U.S. President 15. U.S. Congress 16. U.S. Supreme Court 17. U.S. Federal government 18. Department of Education 19. Council of Chief State Officers 20. National teachers' professional organizations 21. Ad hoc national educational taskforces convened by U.S. President 22. National professional education accreditation/certification boards 23. National education standards boards 24. Federal district judges 25. Secretary of Education 26. Presidential advisors	35. Education experts 36. Teachers' unions 37. Textbook companies 38. National testing companies (CEEB, ETS) 39. Colleges of education 40. National teachers' unions (AFT and NEA) 41. Political action coalitions (PACs) 42. Ad hoc single issue interest/lobby groups 43. Private philanthropic foundations (e.g., Carnegie, Rockefeller, MacArthur, etc.) 44. Corporate business leaders (CEOs) 45. Think tank groups (Brookings, Heritage) 46. Political parties 47. Lobbyists 48. Religious organizations and groups

FIG. 4.3.   Who does or should participate? Groups involved in educational decision making
(reproduce as needed).

Name —————————————————	Course/Section —————————
Observation Site ———————————	Subject ———————————
Date ———————	Other Information —————————

ASSESSING FAMILY–SCHOOL RELATIONSHIPS

Background

An examination of the history of schooling in America provides clear evidence that the separation of the home from the school has a long tradition in public education, dating back to the early Republic period in American history. Mann, for example, thought that poor Irish immigrant parents lacked the moral values, work habits, and social attitudes needed to enculturate their children into the American way of life and industrial work force. Thus, schools were seen as superior and ideal substitutes for the perceived culturally deficient immigrant family culture.[32]

Recent research studies, however, have overwhelmingly demonstrated that where school programs have a strong component of parental involvement, students are consistently better achievers than in otherwise identical programs with less parental involvement.[33] Students in schools that maintain frequent contact with parents consistently outperform other schools. These positive effects persisted, too, well beyond the short term. For example, children of color and those from low-income families who participated in preschool programs with high levels of parent involvement were still outperforming their peers when they reached senior high school.[34]

Although teachers and school administrators often publicly support the importance of greater parental involvement in the schools in official school communiques, the actual performance of American schools in this regard is less impressive. The term *parental involvement*, too, has been subject to a wide variety of interpretations. Does parental involvement mean that parents should be considered expert advisors? willing volunteers? teacher assistants? silent partners? supportive audience? collaborative decision makers? or enthusiastic, day-to-day problem solvers? In the following exercise, you are asked to consider ways that educators can nurture and strengthen the family–school relationship.

Activity

Phase 1. The checklist developed by the staff at the National Committee for Citizens in Education lists some of these new parental involvement initiatives and provides a diagnostic questionnaire that you can use to evaluate how well your host school is working with parents.[35]

Assessing the Family–School Relationship Checklist

(answer "yes" or "no")

Principle 1: School Climate

_____ Do office personnel greet parents (in person or on the phone) in a friendly, courteous way?
_____ Do posted signs warmly welcome parents and visitors?
_____ Are directions written or posted to help parents and visitors to find their way around the school?

_____ Is there a comfortable reception area for parents and visitors equipped with a coat rack and information about the school?

_____ Is there an orientation program for the incoming class of students and their families?

_____ Is there a program for helping mid-year transfer students and their families to settle into the school (e.g., is a staff member assigned to be their host)?

_____ Are there regular social occasions or events at which parents and school staff can get to know each other?

_____ Does the principal have clearly posted office hours when the parents and students can drop in to talk?

_____ Does the school permit parents to observe in class?

_____ Does the school have an "open door" policy that welcomes parents at any time during the school day?

_____ Other?

Principle 2: Communication

_____ Is there a school newsletter with up-to-date information about holidays, special events, and the like?

_____ Does the school send home a calendar listing dates of parent–teacher conferences, report cards, holiday schedules, and major events?

_____ Does the school send home a directory of key Parent–Teacher Association (PTA) representatives and school personnel with phone numbers?

_____ Does the school hold annual back-to-school nights and open houses?

_____ Does the school have a hotline for parents and students to deal with emergencies, rumors, and other burning questions?

_____ Do your policies encourage all teachers to communicate frequently with parents about their curriculum plans, expectations for homework, grading policies, and how they should help?

_____ Do parents know where to go with their concerns, questions, and complaints?

_____ Does the principal review all the school's written communications, including report card format and how test results are reported, to make sure they are respectful of a parent's adult status and yet easy to understand?

_____ Are parents informed of their rights? This includes access to school records, due process in disciplinary actions, and participation in special education decisions.

_____ Other?

Principle 3: Parents as Collaborators and Problem Solvers

_____ Does the school require at least one parent–teacher conference each year for each student?

_____ Does the school offer to set up teacher–parent conferences on request?

_____ Does the school provide in-service training or other opportunities to help teachers communicate and collaborate with parents?

_____ Is there an early warning policy directing teachers to consult with parents promptly if a child is falling behind or having social behavioral problems?

_____ Does the school inform parents right away if a student does not show up for school? Are parents promptly consulted if there is a pattern of unexcused absences?

_____ Does the elementary school confer with parents on the choice of classroom settings or teacher?

_____ Does the high school require parental approval on a student's choice of courses?

_____ Are training and resources (such as a parent advocate) provided for parents of special education students to help them participate in the Individualized Education Plan and other processes?

_____ Other?

Principle 4: Parents as Advisors and Decision Makers

_____ Does the school publish and keep current a policy handbook for parents and students that covers discipline, absences, homework, dress standards, parent and student rights, and so forth?

_____ If the school needs to develop a new policy or program, is there a mechanism for obtaining parental input?

_____ Is there a parent–teacher organization that meets at least once a month?

_____ Do parents ever approach the principal on their own initiative to question school policy or procedures aside from procedures that affect only their child?

_____ When a problem arises at the school, such as a sharp increase in vandalism or drug use or a significant decline in test scores, does the staff inform and enlist the help of parents immediately?

_____ Are there established procedures for dealing with parents' demands, especially those of a vocal minority?

_____ Other?

Principle 5: Outreach to All Families

_____ Is there a policy for informing non-custodial parents about their children's performance and school events?

_____ Do teachers sometimes meet outside school hours with parents who have jobs and cannot easily get away during the working day?

_____ Does the school hold evening and weekend events for its families so that employed parents (mothers, fathers, others) can come to see the school?

_____ If there is a substantial minority language population at the school, are written communications provided in that language?

_____ Is in-service training offered for teachers on how to deal with problems caused by

divorce, separation, or imprisonment, such as how to avoid being caught between warring parents or the impact of family breakup on children?

_____ Are there any special programs, such as peer group discussions, for students whose parents are separating, divorced, imprisoned, or deceased?

_____ Is there an outreach program for parents—especially minority parents—who do not participate at all in school events (e.g., in which faculty or parent volunteers are willing to make home visits or attend local church meetings to answer questions, allay fears, and explain the importance of being involved in their children's education)?

_____ When a particular parent refuses to cooperate with the principal or teacher, is there a school staff member trained to intervene and work with that parent?

_____ Other?

Principle 6: Promoting a Philosophy of Partnership

_____ Does the school have a written statement about partnership with parents that is clearly available, especially in all written publications?

_____ Are there in-service opportunities for training teachers to work with parents?

_____ Is time at staff meetings devoted to discussing working with parents and reinforcing efforts of teachers and parents?

_____ Are teachers encouraged to consult with the principal if they are having difficulty dealing with a parent?

_____ Does the principal offer to sit in at meetings with teachers and parents or to mediate any dispute between them?

_____ Does the principal substitute in the classroom or make substitutes available

_____ to allow teachers and other staff to have meetings with parents?

_____ Does the school offer assistance to help parents with babysitting, transportation, or other logistical difficulties so they can attend school events?

_____ Are space, staff support, and resources (i.e., reasonable access to a copy machine, computer services, a desk, etc.) provided for parents' school-related activities?

_____ Other?

Principle 7: Volunteer Participation

_____ Does the school have an organized volunteer program with a coordinator (paid or volunteer)?

_____ Does the program draw from retired people, the business community, local citizens, and students as well as parents?

_____ Is there a wide variety of jobs available for volunteers including ones that could be done at home or on the weekends?

_____ Are all parents expected to volunteer in some way during the school year?

_____ Is the program reassessed periodically, with the participation of parents, teachers, and other volunteers, to ensure that the program is meeting school needs effectively?

_____ Are local businesses and community organizations contacted to provide learning opportunities outside the school and to explore career options for high school students?

_____ Has a local business (or other institutions) been asked to "adopt" your school?

_____ Other?

Phase 2. The following suggested activities are designed to help you complete a final assessment of your host school's family–school relationships, especially from the perspective of the many barriers that parents face in their attempts to become more involved in their children's education:

1. Take a snapshot or draw a picture of the entrance to the school. Examine it carefully. Does the school look inviting, friendly, and homey? How do you think that parents of different cultural or class groups would tend to "read" the school entrance? What architectural features present physical barriers between parents and schools?

2. Now, take a second snapshot or draw a picture of the school's main office. Examine it carefully. Does the school's main office look inviting and friendly? Is there a special room for parents at the school? Is anyone in the school specially assigned to make parents feel welcome? How were you greeted when you came into the office? Is there any official protocol established in the school to deal with parental visits? Are translators available for parents who do not speak English? What are parents and other visitors required to do when they enter the school? Sit in the office for an hour. Make note of the interaction between parents and school personnel.

3. Make a list of all the special events held at the school during the year that include parents. When are these events held? How are they advertised? Are parents invited individually? Is child care and transportation provided for these events? How does the school communicate with the parents? What messages do school policies give to parents about their acceptance in the daily life of school? Are some groups of parents more welcome in the school than are other groups? How does the scheduling of open houses, PTA meetings, and conferences prevent some parents from being more involved in the school?

4. Attend a PTA meeting. Make a tally by both race and gender of those who attend. Find out how PTA officers are elected. In what activities is the PTA involved? Interview the head of the PTA and ask her or him to construct a similar list of the ways that she or he conceptualizes the idea of parental involvement.

Reflective Narrative

Now look more critically at the information that you have gathered. Have any of your findings surprised you? On a separate page, make a list of the areas you determine to be special strengths at the schools and those that need more work. Discuss your findings with a school administrator.

Related Readings

Berger, E. H. (2003). *Parents as partners in education: Families and schools working together* (6th ed.). Upper Saddle River, NJ: Prentice-Hall.

Comer, J. P. (1980). *Schoolpower: Implications of an intervention project.* New York: Free Press.

Daher, J. (1994). *School–parent partnerships: A guide.* In C. Fagnano & B. Weber (Eds.), *School, family, and community interaction: A view from the firing lines* (pp. 111–130). Boulder, CO: Westview.

DeCarvelho, M. E. P. (2000). *Rethinking family–school relations: A critique of parental involvement in schooling.* Mahwah, NJ: Lawrence Erlbaum Associates.

Epstein, J. (2002). *School, family, and community partnerships: Your handbook for action* (2nd ed.). Thousand Oaks, CA: Corwin.

Gestwicki, C. (2003). *Home, school, and community relations: A guide to working with families.* Albany, NY: Thomson/Delmar.

Henderson, A. T. (1986). *Beyond the bake sale: An educator's guide to working with parents.* Washington, DC: National Committee for Citizens in Education.

Olsen, G. W., & Fuller, M. L. (Eds.). (2002). *Home-school relations: Working successfully with parents and families.* Needham, MA: Allyn & Bacon.

Ryan, B. A., Adams, G. R., Gullotta, T., Weissberg, R., & Hampton, R. (Eds.). (1995). *The family–school connection: Theory, research, and practice.* Thousand Oaks, CA: Sage.

Trumbull, E., Greenfield, P. M., Rothstein-Fish, C., & Quiroz, B. (2001). *Bridging cultures between home and school: A guide for teachers.* Mahwah, NJ: Lawrence Erlbaum Associates.

Winters, W. C. (1993). *African American mothers and urban schools: The power of participation.* New York: Lexington.

Wittreich, Y. M., Jacobi, E., Hogue, I., & Hogue, E. (2003). *Getting parents involved: A handbook of ideas for teachers, schools, and communities.* Norwood, MA: Christopher-Gordon.

ASSESSING THE PARENT–TEACHER RELATIONSHIP

Background

The involvement of parents in the school has been found to be an important indicator of student success.[36] Recent educational research studies have overwhelmingly confirmed the psychological, social, and academic benefits of greater parental involvement and participation at every level of their children's elementary, middle, and high school education.[37] Given the demands of parental work schedules today (regardless of social class), most parents find it difficult (if not impossible) to be physically involved in their children's schools, especially during normal school hours. Research has also shown, however, that parents of all social classes want to be more involved in their children's education but seek more direction from the classroom teacher.[38] Teachers themselves feel ambivalent about the wisdom of encouraging greater parental involvement in the schools, and only about 47% of inner city teachers surveyed believed in strong family involvement.[39] As a result, schools have begun to see the value of more in-service teacher education programs focusing on parental involvement and have begun to experiment with many innovative and creative parental involvement programs and practices.

In the following exercise you will be invited to examine the nature and scope of parent–teacher relationships at your host school from the perspective of the many barriers that parents face. Consider the following questions. Despite the growing body of research literature that catalogs the effectiveness of parental involvement programs, are the parent–teacher connections at your host school either nonexistent or confined to periodic, superficial "displays" of parental support (i.e., the annual PTA meeting, meet-the-teacher nights, and end-of-year awards ceremonies)? Are there any school and teacher practices that deter further parental involvement? What is meant by the term *parental involvement* at your host school?

Activity

The following checklist developed by the staff at the National Committee for Citizens in Education lists some new parental involvement initiatives and provides a diagnostic questionnaire that you can use to evaluate how well your host school is fostering healthy parent–teacher relationships.[40]

Assessing Parent–Teacher Relationships Checklist

(answer "yes" or "no")

Principle 1: Classroom Climate

_____ Are parent observers welcome in the classroom?

_____ Are there any adult-sized chairs besides the teacher's?

_____ Is the classroom organized so that a parent can easily see what happens in it?

_____ Are examples of every child's work displayed regularly?

_____ Is the classroom routine written down and clearly posted?

_____ Are parents worked with from an empowerment rather than a deficit model of parental involvement?

_____ Other?

Principle 2: Communication

_____ Are parents informed at the beginning of the year how they can reach the teacher?

_____ Does the teacher tell parents about the good things as well as problems?

_____ Does the teacher try to communicate at least once a month with each parent (less often in high school, but regularly)?

_____ Does the teacher talk to parents in person (or on the phone) in addition to sending written messages or e-mails?

_____ Does the teacher provide regular opportunities for parents to see their child's written work?

_____ Does the teacher let parents know of expectations for homework, grading policies, and how parents can help?

_____ Does the teacher let parents know what information about the child is needed to help teachers do a better job (e.g., family stress or major changes in family: illness, birth, death, divorce, etc.).

_____ Does the teacher praise parents regularly in front of peers at group meetings?

_____ Other?

Principle 3: Parents as Collaborators

_____ Do teachers ask parents for their advice on how to deal with their children?

_____ Is there an early warning system for notifying parents if a student is falling behind or having social problems so the teacher may confer with them about the situation?

_____ Before parents are informed about a serious problem, are other school staff consulted to gather their perspectives on the student?

_____ Are parents encouraged to advise teachers when a child is exhibiting a learning or school adjustment difficulty at home?

_____ In suggesting ways that parents can help at home, does the teacher take into account a student's particular cultural background and home situation?

_____ Do teachers make it clear to parents that parents must respect their need for time alone and with their own families?

_____ Do teachers help parents understand that their child's needs must be balanced with those of the whole class?

_____ Are parents employed in the classrooms as teacher's aides? tutors? counselors? chaperons? hall monitors? or assistants in the computer labs or library?

_____ Are parents invited to speak to the class about their careers, their hobbies, and the like?

_____ Other?

Principle 4: Parents as Advisors and Decision Makers

_____ Are parents with questions and ideas about school policy encouraged to play an active role in the school as members of advisory boards?

_____ Do teachers attend parent–teacher organization meetings regularly?

_____ Do teachers listen actively to parents' concerns and pass them on to the principal or the parent–teacher organization president?

_____ Do teachers make it clear that some decisions about a child are not negotiable (e.g., grades? promotions? what else?).

_____ Other?

Principle 5: Outreach to All Families

_____ Are teachers adequately trained and supported in their dealings with the problems of divorced or separated families?

_____ Do teachers make special efforts to reach families from other cultures (e.g., home visits, translators, etc.)?

_____ Do teachers meet outside regular school hours, if necessary, with parents who are employed?

_____ Are teachers persistent in their efforts to reach parents who try to avoid coming to school?

_____ Do teachers invite parents to eat breakfast and lunch with their children at school?

_____ Other?

Principle 6: Volunteers

_____ Do teachers use volunteers creatively (both parents and other citizens) to meet needs in the classroom?

_____ Do teachers expect every parent to help in some way, and are parents offered a variety of ways to do so?

_____ Other?

Reflective Narrative

What further implications and recommendations might you draw from your findings? The report *A Nation of Risk*[41] and other similar reform documents have tended to acknowledge the primacy of parental participation in "the work of the schools," emphasizing the role of parents in the achievement of national- and state-level curriculum content, subject standards, disciplinary expectations, skill basics, and standardized testing. By contrast, Epstein,[42] at the Center for Research on Effective Schooling for Disadvantaged Students, has argued thus:

[P]erhaps the ideal situation for children's education and development occurs, when school–family distinctions become blurred—when schools become more family-like and families become more school-like.[42]

Martin presents the imagery of the "school-home," a place characterized by "safety, security, nurturance, and love … [and] guided by a spirit of family-like affection."[43] Which model characterizes the school climate at your host school? Do you agree or disagree with Epstein's and Martin's images for the American school? Why or why not? What is your vision of the ideal teacher–parent relationship?

Related Readings

Comer, J. P. (1980). *Schoolpower: Implications of an intervention project*. New York: Free Press.

Dodd, A. W., & Konzai, J. L. (2000). *Making our high schools better: How parents and teachers can work together*. New York: St. Martins Press.

Henderson, A. T. (1986). *Beyond the bake sale: An educator's guide to working with parents*. Washington, DC: National Committee for Citizens in Education.

Morrow, R. D. (1989). Southeast Asian parent involvement: Can it be a reality? *Elementary School Guidance and Counseling, 23*, 289–297.

Noddings, N. (1992). *The challenge to care in schools: An alternative approach to education*. New York: Teachers College Press.

Rockwell, R. E. (1995). *Parents and teachers as partners: Issues and challenges*. Albany, NY: Thomson Learning.

Vincent, C. (1996). *Parents and teachers: Power and participation*. New York: Falmer.

Winter, W. C. (1993). *African American mothers and urban schools: The power of participation*. New York: Lexington.

SCHOOL-TO-WORK LINKAGES

Background

There are few more controversial issues today in U.S. education than the role of the schools in preparing students for the world of work. This is not as much of a problem for upwardly mobile, middle-class, college-bound youngsters as it is for poor, minority, at-risk students. The latter students many times feel a hopelessness about never having the kind of job that will provide them with stable employment and the resources to provide for a secure family household. Current labor force analyses have highlighted the difficulties encountered by these young people in making the transition from school to work.[44]

The scarcity of stable, low-credentialed employment in the United States has made it almost impossible for these working-class students to find good-paying career jobs right after high school. Research reveals that they tend to spend several years floundering in the labor market, and many do not succeed in finding steady work until the age of 40 years.[45] These concerns, along with the extraordinary workplace benefits and salary differentials of workers with college degrees, have raised serious questions about the kind of vocational education programs needed in the 21st century.

Stern and his associates[46] classified school-to-work programs into two categories: school-for-work programs (i.e., the older, more traditional vocational education programs) and school-and-work programs (i.e., the newer programs that have been more comprehensively integrated with the academic school curricula).

The school-for-work programs generally are those vocational programs funded under the Smith–Hughes Act of 1917 that emphasize the need to train workers in the industrial intelligence and mechanical skills needed by routine, assembly-line production systems. These school-for-work programs have long suffered from the reputation of being the dumping grounds for children experiencing difficulty with the regular classroom academic programs (i.e., academically underachieving students, resistant lower class minority children with behavior problems, and mentally challenged students). When the dramatic loss in manufacturing jobs took place in the late 1970s and early 1980s, these school-for-work programs shifted from a manufacturing emphasis to that of training youth for the emerging fast-food, transportation, and restaurant enterprises.[47]

Some would argue that although these new service sector jobs are unsuitable for college-bound, middle-class youth (except on a temporary basis), they are ideal for lower class, nonacademic youth. Indeed, minorities are highly represented in these occupations (more than 22% of employees in eating establishments are Black or Hispanic). From another perspective, however, it is argued that these jobs provide little opportunity for job mobility and offer little room for initiative, creativity, or individual expression. Etizoni wrote that these "fast-food franchises are breeding grounds for robots working for yesterday's assembly lines and not practice fields for committed workers in tomorrow's high-tech posts."[48] Not only do these workplaces provide

111

meager income and few useful job skills for these youth, but they also tend to perpetuate their disadvantaged status: Such jobs provide no career incentives and few marketable skills.[49] No wonder there is growing concern among vocational educators about what and how they are teaching these students.

Data suggest that although this older model of vocational education is still the predominant model used in American schools, there is a shift toward the newer school-and-work programs. The Carl D. Perkins Vocational and Applied Technology Education Act of 1990 called for the integration of vocational and academic education through school-and-work programs that allow students to work and attend class during the same time period. Cooperative education, new youth apprenticeships, and school-based enterprises are the major examples of these work programs being offered to students in many high schools and secondary vocational centers. The most positive aspect of such programs is that academic skills, critical-thinking skills, and problem-solving skills are considered equally important as any specific occupational skill training. There is also a priority that these programs provide students with the academic credentials to pursue either college-level studies or types of postsecondary education.[50]

Activity

Using the chart from Fig. 4.4, investigate the vocational education programs at your host school. Take note of the defining characteristics of the students in these classes. What can you conclude about the age, race, ethnicity, sex, and academic characteristics of these students?

Speak with some of the vocational education teachers about their programs and their students. Have they seen a shift in emphasis in the programs over the past 15 years? If so, what has been the nature of the changes in the programs? What has been the impact of these programs on the students? Are they satisfied with the voca-

tional education program at their school? What would they do to improve it?

Find out how many of the following strategies are currently being used at the school in which you are doing your classroom observations to prepare all students better for the school-to-work transition.

Reflective Narrative

Although applauding the direction of these newer vocational education programs with their increased concern for the academic as well as applied vocational and technology programs, some critical theorists are concerned that vocational education students still lack the kind of entry-level knowledge and skills needed to ensure that they can "interject their social and moral imaginations into the refashioning of work—where workplace ethics, economics, and politics are defined not by cultural elites, but by a consensus of the whole."[51] Lakes[52] argued strongly for a "critical education for work" that would enable future vocational education students to reexamine the assumptions on which their programs rest. What do you think are the components of a critical education for work for vocational education students?

Related Readings

Borman, K. (1991). *The first "real" job: A study of young workers*. Albany: State University of New York Press.

Lakes, R. D. (Ed.). (1994). *Critical education and work: Multidisciplinary approaches*. Norwood, NJ: Ablex.

Law, C. J., & Knuth, R. A. , & Bergman, S. (1992). *What does research say about school-to-work transition?* Oak Brook, IL: NCREL; Electric Library, WWW.

Rifkin, J. (1995). *The end of work: The decline of the global labor force and the dawn of the post-market era*. New York: Putnam.

Simon, R. I., Dippo, D., & Schenke, A. (1991). *Learning work: A critical pedagogy of work education*. New York: Bergin & Garvey.

Opportunities for Students	Yes	No
1. To learn outside of school		
2. To have access to adults in the community as role models, tutors, or mentors		
3. To provide service learning and community service activities such as volunteer work, environmental clean-ups, home building projects, disaster relief efforts, and the like		
4. To join local community business and organizational clubs to develop mentoring relationships and job networks		
5. To hear community business leaders discuss the nature of their occupations, their challenges, and work motivations		
6. To visit a variety of local community businesses and corporate centers to see work skills in operation in the real world		
7. To investigate via action research projects local businesses, industries, and service sector agencies to familiarize themselves with job requirements and work culture in local establishments		
8. To participate in career training programs and apprenticeships that span both secondary and postsecondary education		
9. To select from a variety of vocational training opportunities including tech-prep programs, school-based enterprises, co-op programs, and the like		
10. To develop advanced technical and basic academic skills that lead to a high school diploma		
11. To consult with job placement and counseling services for students that are open ended and developmental in nature		
12. To have access to a well-established job placement office that provides, encourages, and plans on-campus job interviews with prospective employers through career days, job fairs, and career information workshops		
13. To attend college-linked technical training programs at school that provide college credit		

FIG. 4.4. Survey of School-to-Work Linkages[51]

EXTRACURRICULAR SCHOOL ACTIVITIES

Background

In studies of schooling and youth culture in the United States, the role and function of extracurricular school activities has been a rich subject for historical and sociological study. Although researchers are divided on their analyses of the function that extracurricular activities has played and continues to play in the larger community life of the nation, there is little disagreement that extracurricular school activities do contribute to the development and reinforcement of a wide array of physical, emotional, social, academic, aesthetic, and spiritual dimensions of a young child. In addition to the feeling of belonging, so important for children, extracurricular school activities take the place of negative peer influences and "the TV-till-bedtime routine" so common among many American children.

In recent historical studies, O'Hanlon,[53] Spring,[54] Violas,[55] and others[56] have researched the history of extracurricular sports in U.S. schools. They have discovered that Progressive Era extracurricular school activities were initially adopted into the public school curriculum to fill the vacant time (especially of poor urban children) with supervised after-school activities designed to reinforce the new group-oriented, assembly-line industrial work habits and attitudes (i.e., group competition, unequal rewards, and hard work, etc.) in working-class, immigrant children. In his research, Spring[57] emphasized "the unification function" that extracurricular activities played in the new comprehensive high schools by creating a dominant school cultural ethos characterized by "school spirit," teamwork, and "working for the good of the whole." Spring questioned whether extracurricular school activities do or should play such a role in the public school systems. In addition, some concern exists that such programs function to mitigate feelings of class consciousness or tendencies toward social class conflict in the schools in light of the concomitant adoption and implementation by school administrators of hierarchical systems of student academic tracking and standardized testing.

Today, the issue of extracurricular school activities is equally problematic and subject to varying interpretations. Sociologists are divided on the present role and function that extracurricular sports activities play in today's school culture.[58] Some believe that films, television, Nintendo, video arcades, and computer games have taken the place of extracurricular sports for many youngsters. Others believe that nothing has really replaced the character-building potential of extracurricular sports and that increased teenage violence and crime rates may be directly related to our neglect of the centrality that extracurricular sports should have for all our children, not just the elite few.

Given the renewed emphasis on "the basics" combined with increasingly financially strapped school districts, many schools are now curtailing extracurricular school activities as unnecessary frills. Increasing numbers of high school students are involved in after-school service sector jobs until late in the evening.[59] In many schools, too, after-school activities have died a slow death—largely due to scheduling conflicts with buses, general student apathy, and the growing tendency to professionalize after-school activities.[60] It is crucial, therefore, that the beginning teacher educator examine the status, vitality, and breadth of extracurricular school activities at their host schools.

Activity

What extracurricular activities did you participate in when you were in high school? Describe the students who participated with you in these activities by social class, gender, and race or ethnicity.

Using the chart from Fig. 4.5, make a list of all the extracurricular activities available to students at the school. Get a list of times and places that each team, club, or activity meets. Make an attempt to attend at least one meeting of each school team, club, or activity. During the meeting, make some notes about the composition of the club in terms of the students' perceived social class, racial, ethnic, gender, or academic-track characteristics. Attempt to solicit some qualitative comments from the participants about why they joined this particular club and whether other members of their peer group also joined the club.

Reflective Narrative

Phase One.

1. On the basis of your notes, what general conclusions might you draw about the status, vitality, inclusive nature, and breadth of extracurricular activities at your school?
2. Check your impressions with one of the school administrators. What recommendations might you make to the school administration to ensure more equitable participation by all races, genders, and ability classes in each extracurricu-

lar activity? Develop your own rationale for the importance of extracurricular sports and extracurricular school activities.

Phase Two.   Now, review the survey data you have generated regarding extracurricular activities at your school from a more critical and analytic perspective. How do you explain the similarities or differences that you found from the school you attended as a child? In drawing your comparisons, ask yourself the following questions:

1. Who participates in extracurricular activities at your host school? Do you think there might be a hidden set of rules and assumptions about who should show up for certain sports or specific after-school activities at your school? Thus, is there an issue of access and students' perceptions about the race, ethnicity, gender, physical makeup, academic credentials, social status, and so on of the students likely to be accepted if they show up for certain activities?
2. Do extracurricular activities tend to be class based at your host school? Often, extracurricular sports activities function only to reproduce the same social class and ethnic differences evident in the school's academic tracking systems (i.e., nerds in newspaper club; jocks in sports clubs; middle class in large group activities—band, service club, etc.; ivy leaguers in solo sports—swimming, kayaking, chess, etc.). Is this the case at the school?
3. What groups do not participate in extracurricular activities at your host school? It is also important to notice what groups are routinely missing from any kind of participation in extracurricular sports (e.g., the greasers, the punks, the druggies, the skinheads, the at-risk students, etc.). This disaffected population of potential dropouts often form their own after-school groups. What might the school do to include these groups in some meaningful after-school activities?
4. Review your host school's student handbook for the policies concerning extracurricular

sports. Are there prescribed requirements for participation and training? What are they? Are there explicit prohibitions against the possession or use of illegal substances? Do certain sports require that students participate in a insurance program or have written parental approval? Which ones? Why? Do all the extracurricular groups and clubs hold award ceremonies at the end of the year? Are only a few students given awards or does every student who participates receive a certificate of participation? Which extracurricular activities hold competitions with other schools? What is the transportation policy for traveling to and from school sponsored activities?

Related Readings

Holloway, J. H. (1999). Extracurricular activities: The path to academic success? *Educational Leadership, 57*(4), December 1999–January 2000, pp. 87–88. Retrieved June 29, 2005, from http://www.education-world.com/a_curr/curr237.shtml

O-Hanlon, T. (1980). Interscholastic Athletics, 1900–1940: Shaping citizens for unequal roles in the modern industrial state. *Educational Theory, 30,* 89–103.

Spring, J. (1972). *Education and the rise of the corporate liberal state.* Boston: Beacon Press.

Violas, P. (1978). *The training of the urban working class: A history of twentieth century American education* (pp. 93–123). Chicago: Rand McNally.

Listing of Extracurricular Activities	Frequency of Meetings	# Enrolled Students	Students' Economic Status (L-M-U)	Students' Racial Composition	Students' Gender	Students' Academic Track
1. Athletic Teams/Clubs (Types?)						
2. Band/Orchestra						
3. Choir/Choral Clubs						
4. Career-Oriented Clubs (Types?)						
5. Language Clubs (Types?)						
6. Drama/Theater						
7. Pep Club/Spirit Band						
8. School Publications						
9. Student Council/ Government						
10. Service/Volunteer Groups						
11. National Honor Societies						
12. Debate/Speech						
13. Cheerleading						
14. Science Clubs						
15. Radio/Broadcasting Clubs						
16. Computer Clubs						
17. Math Club						
18. Music Lessons						
19. Writing/Poetry Groups						
20. Gymnastics/Physical Fitness Activities						
21. Painting/Art/ Photography Classes						
22. Extracurricular School Trips						
23. Modern Dance/Ballet						
24. Culture Clubs						
25. Other						
26. Other						
27. Other						

FIG. 4.5. Student participation in school-related activities (reproduce as needed).

VIOLENT SCHOOLS?—SAFE SCHOOLS?

Background

The media (i.e., films, TV, radio broadcasts, videos, music stations, books, magazines, newspaper stories, etc.) bombards the public every day with accounts of child abuse, rape, missing children, murder, robbery, juvenile crime, drug busts, gun shows and the like feeding the fear that much of the American public already has for their own personal safety. Shooting incidents that have taken place in Springfield, Oregon; Jonesboro, Arkansas; Pearl, Mississippi; and Columbine, Colorado have combined to create a perception that school crime and violence has also reached record highs. Although our statistics show that the actual occurrence of death in school is much lower than the media portrays, there is little doubt that America has become a more dangerous place for a young person to live. Not surprisingly, the American public school has become a focus of efforts to reduce school crime and violence. Consider the following statistics:[61]

America and Gun Violence

- Every day more than 80 Americans die from gun violence. (Coalition to Stop Gun Violence, 2004; NEA Health Information Network/School and Community Safety web page, 2005)
- As of 1994, 44 million Americans owned more than 192 million firearms, 65 million of which were handguns. Although there were enough guns to have provided every U.S. adult with one, only 25% of adults owned firearms. Seventy-four percent (74%) of gun owners possessed two or more firearms. (National Institute of Justice, May 1997).

Children and Gun Violence

- American children are more at risk from firearms than children of any other industrialized nation. In one year, firearms killed no children in Japan, 19 in Great Britain, 57 in Germany, 109 in France, 153 in Canada, and 5,285 in the United States. (Centers for Disease Control and Protection, 1997).
- The rate of firearm deaths among children under 15 is almost 12 times higher than in 25 other industrialized countries combined (Centers for Disease Control and Protection, 1997).
- Nation wide for 2002, gun violence killed 2,893 American children and teens ages 19 and under, a decrease of 1% from the nationwide 2001 total of 2,937. While these numbers have been steadily decreasing over the past five years, an average of 8 young people killed every day by guns in the U.S. is still too many. That is one child every three hours, eight children every day, and more than 50 children every week. (Centers for Disease Control National Center for Health Statistics mortality report, 2005).

American Schools, Children and School Violence

Key findings on school crime and safety have been published in a recent report *Indicators of School Crime and Safety: 2004* released by the U.S. Department of Education and the U.S. Department of Justice:

- Between 1992 and 2002, the total crime rate for students ages 12 to 18, as well as rates of theft and violent crimes declined. (*Indicators of School Crime and Safety: 2004*, 2004).

- Despite the high profile shootings at schools like Columbine High School in Littleton, Colorado, school shootings account for a very small percentage of all youth firearm deaths. From 1993-1998, fewer than 1% of all firearm deaths among young people ages 5 to 9 occurred in schools. (Miller, M., Azrael, D., & Hemenway, D. *The Journal of Trauma*, 2002).

- Still, many young people apparently have little difficulty obtaining guns, either from home, from friends, through illegal purchase from gun dealers or "on the street," or through theft. A study published in the *American Journal of Public Health* in 2000 found that an estimated 34% of children in the United States live in homes with firearms. (*American Journal of Public Health*, 2000).

- In addition, a national study of male high school sophomores and juniors conducted in 1998 by the National Institute of Justice Research founded that 50% of respondents reported that obtaining a gun would be "little" or "no" trouble. (National Institute of Justice Research, 1998).

- Between 1993 and 2003, the percentage of students in grades 9–12 who reported carrying a weapon such as a gun, knife, or cub on school property within the previous 30 days dropped by half, from 12 to 6 percent. (*Indicators of School Crime and Safety: 2004*, 2004).

- More than 3,500 students were expelled in 1998-99 for bringing guns to school. Of these, 43% were in elementary or junior high school. This means that, in a 40 week school year, an average of 88 children per week nationwide are expelled for bringing a gun in schools. And these figures include only the children who get caught. (*U.S. Department of Education Report on State Implementation of the Gun-Free Schools Act, School Year 1998–99*, October 2000).

- Between 1993 and 2003, the percentage of students in grades 9–12 who reported being in a fight on school property declined from 16 percent to 13 percent. (*Indicators of School Crime and Safety: 2004*, 2004).

- In 2003, students in grades 9–12 were asked about using drugs on school property. In the 30 days prior to the survey, 5 percent of students reported having at least one drink of alcohol on school property and 6 percent reported using marijuana. (*Indicators of School Crime and Safety: 2004*, 2004).

Bullying and Hate-Related Graffiti

- In 2003, 7 percent of students ages 12 to 18 reported that they had been bullied at school. The percentage of students in this age range who had been bullied increased from 5 percent in 1999 to 8 percent in 2001, but no difference was detected between 2001 and 2003. (*Indicators of School Crime and Safety: 2004*, 2004).

- In 2003, 12 percent of students aged 12–18 reported that someone at school had used hate-related words against them (i.e., derogatory words related to race, religion, ethnicity, disability, gender, or sexual orientation). During the same period, about 36 percent of students ages 12 and 18 saw hate-related graffiti at school. (*Indicators of School Crime and Safety: 2004*, 2004).

Children and Media Violence

- By age 18, the average American child will have viewed 200,000 acts of violence on television alone. (American Academy of Pediatrics, *Understanding the impact of media on children and teens*, 2004).
- A 2002 national TV violence study found that nearly 2 out of 3 TV programs contained some violence, averaging about 6 violent acts per hour. (Kaiser Family Foundation, *Key Facts: TV Violence*, Spring, 2003).
- Average time per week that the American child ages 2–17 spends watching television: 19 hours, 40 minutes (Nielson, *Media Research*, 2000).
- Hours of TV watching per week shown to negatively affect academic achievement: 10 hours or more (U.S. Department of Education, *Strong families, strong schools: Building community partnerships for learning*, 1994:1).
- Time per day that TV is on in an average U.S. home: 7 hours, 40 minutes. (Nielson, *Media Research*, 2000).
- Hours per year the average American youth spends in school: 900 Hours per year the average American youth watches television: 1,023 (Barber, B. *Harper's*, Nov. 1993:41; Nielson, *Media Research*, 2000).

Children who watch a lot of TV news tend to overestimate the prevalence of crime and may perceive the world to be a more dangerous place than it actually is. (Smith, S., & Wilson, B., 2002).

Given these statistics, it is understandable why the creation of a safe and orderly school environment has become a major research and media emphasis in recent school reform efforts. A growing body of research has suggested that school practices can be effective in dealing with these disruptive student behaviors. The research is divided, however, on the causes and probable solutions to this recent rapid escalation of school violence and criminal activity.[62]

Police Model of School Security

Proponents of this model argue that school violence has resulted from the growing presence of criminal and gang-related activities within the public school grounds. They recommend the installation of massive electronic surveillance and security systems. This police model of school security recommends implementing the following measures in response to increased school violence and destruction of school property:

1. Increased high-tech surveillance (e.g., video cameras, metal detectors, two-way radios, mirrors, X-ray machines, phones in classrooms, closed-circuit TV, etc.).
2. Tougher discipline (e.g., imposing stricter dress codes, requiring school uniforms, creating "zero tolerance" schools, etc.).
3. Increased student locker searches and use of drug-detecting dogs.
4. Creation of gun-free school zones.
5. More school security personnel including school resource officers, probation officers, and school-linked police. (The New York City school system now operates the 11th largest security force in the United States, with more than 2,400 officers.)
6. Tougher punishment (e.g., more school infractions that require suspension and expulsion proceedings) and tighter connections with the juvenile court system and alternative education placement programs.
7. Increased use of "yellow-code alerts" alongside fire drills so that children learn to "hit the deck when the bullets fly."[63]
8. Completing criminal background checks on teachers and staff.
9. Fencing school grounds.
10. Installing bulletproof school windows.
11. Designating one main door entry to school and locking all others to outside entry.
12. Requiring photo identification badges for students and staff and identification cards for all school visitors.

13. School security as a school goal alongside academic achievement.[64]

Ecology/Climate Model of School Security

By contrast, the ecology/climate model of school security frames school security within the wider context of overcrowded classrooms, school segregation, student poverty, and racial tension. This approach to school security argues that when educators blame only youth gangs for school violence, they prevent themselves from seeking a more comprehensive approach to creating a truly safe and academic learning environment. In contrast to the police model that focuses on the characteristics of counterculture school groups, the ecology model emphasizes the importance of improving the learning environment by concentrating on the school's climate, wellness, culture, and organizational features. For example, the National Institute of Education report[65] recommends the following measures as a way to eliminate school violence:

1. Reinforce the vision that all students can learn, study, and work peacefully together. Care and consideration must be extended to each person within the school environment.
2. School processes, practices, and organizational structures need to provide a strong learning environment free of racial tension or discrimination based on race, gender, language, and the like.
3. School restructuring needs to encourage greater use of student and administrative dialogues, greater voice for students in the school's operation, and increased student participation in all aspects of school decision making.
4. A sense of community must be developed; parental and neighborhood ties must be strengthened; parents must be made partners and decision makers in every aspect of the school's operation.
5. School facilities must be better maintained and upgraded.[66]
6. Recruit community members to provide safe houses along school routes and safe afterschool care programs for all the community's schoolchildren.
7. Provide closer supervision, particularly in stressful situations or those in which bullying is likely to happen.
8. Provide nonviolent communication and conflict-resolution programs aimed at helping students accept difference, tolerate diversity, and resolve conflicts in creative and nonviolent ways.

Activity

Study the model of school security in operation at your school. Does it resemble the police model or the ecology/climate model? Discuss each of these models with members of the school administration. Get their views on why they prefer and use one rather than the other.

Reflective Narrative

Politicians are often known for finding and using statistics that justify whatever social policy they chose to support. The crime statistics are no exception, especially as they relate to increased rates of school violence, gang-related school activities, and school property damage. Put yourself in the role of a critically skeptical educational researcher. Is there any way you can independently verify or critique the statistics presented in this exercise? Are there any more up-to-date sources that might change one's perspective on these issues? (Hint: You might want to consult the following Internet sites: Center for the Prevention of School Violence and/or SchoolNet.)

Related Readings

Teachers' Guide/Bowling for Columbine Web site. (2003). Retrieved July 7, 2005, from http://

www.bowlingforcolumbine.com/library/teachers/pdf/complete.pdf

Bey, T. M., & Turner, G. Y. (1995). *Making school a place of peace*. Thousand Oaks, CA: Corwin Press.

Brown, M. (2003). After Columbine: Preventing and responding to school violence. In C. Shea & W. S. Thomson (Eds.), *Teacher's manual for North Carolina educators* (pp. 218–225). New York: McGraw-Hill.

Curicio, J. L., & First, P. F. (1993). *Violence in the schools: How to proactively prevent and defuse it*. Newbury Park, CA: Corwin Press.

DiGiulio, R. (2001). *Educate, medicate, or litigate?: What teachers, parents, and administrators must do about student behavior*. Thousand Oaks, CA: Corwin Press.

Fishbaugh, M. S., & Hill, F. W. (1994). *Creating safe schools: What principals can do*. Thousand Oaks, CA: Corwin Press.

Goodwille, S. (Ed.). (1993). *Voices from the future: Our children tell us about violence in America*. New York: Crown.

Knowles, C. R. (2001). *Prevention that works!: A guide for developing school-based drug and violence prevention programs*. Thousand Oaks, CA: Corwin Press.

National Center for Children Exposed to Violence. (2004, June 14). *School violence*. Retrieved June 28, 2005, from http://www.nccew.org/violence/school.html

National Center for Children Exposed to Violence. (2004, June 14). *Media violence*. Retrieved June 28, 2005, from http://www.nccev.org/violence/media.html

National Center for Children Exposed to Violence. (2004, June 14). *Catastrophic events*. Retrieved June 28, 2005, from http://www.nccev.org/violence/events.html

National Criminal Justice Reference Service. (2005, March 1). *School safety—Facts and figures*. Retrieved July 10, 2005, from http://www.ncjrs.org/school_safety/summary.html

National Education Association (Health and Information Network, School and Community Safety) Web site. (2005, April 14). *Statistics: Gun violence in our communities*. Retrieved June 29, 2005, from http://www.neahin.org/program/schoolsafety/gunsafety/statistics.htm

National Institute of Education. (1978). *Violent schools—safe schools: The safe school study, report to Congress, Volume I*. Washington, DC: Government Printing Office.

National School Board Association. (1994). *Violence in our schools: How America's school boards are safeguarding your children*. Washington, DC: Author.

National Strategy Forum. (2004, March). *School safety in the 21st century: Adapting to new security challenges post-9/11*. Retrieved July 10, 2005, from http://www.nassleo.org/news/finalpublpdf

National Youth Violence Prevention Campaign. (2005, July 8). *General violence prevention*. Retrieved July 10, 2005, from http://www.violencepreventionweek.org/index.html?menu=resources&1=6

National Youth Violence Prevention Campaign. (2005, July 8). *Bullying prevention*. Retrieved July 10, 2005, from http://www.violencepreventionweek.org/index.html?menu=resources&1=12

North Carolina Center for the Prevention of School Violence. (2005, July 8, 2005). *School Violence Statistics*. Retrieved July 10, 2005, from http://www.ncdjjdp.org/cpsv/library/statistics.htm

North Carolina Public School Forum. (2003). Safe schools. In C. Shea & W. S. Thomson (Eds.), *Teacher's manual for North Carolina educators* (pp. 206–217). New York: McGraw-Hill.

Quarles, C. L. (1993). *Staying safe at school*. Thousand Oaks, CA: Corwin Press.

CYBERSPACE, DIGITAL AGE EQUITY, AND THE VIRTUAL CLASSROOM

Background

We can not afford to leave behind any of our children in this Information Age. Failure to bridge the gap will relegate our sons and daughters to sit in the backseat of the technology train on the Information Superhighway.
—(Maxine Waters (D-CA, 2002).[67]

The unfortunate reality of our high-tech society is the tremendous information and communication gap, the "digital divide" that exists for many groups of American citizens. Only by providing equitable and meaningful access to technology can we ensure that all children step into the 21st century together. However, recent studies have revealed that the digital divide is growing between the haves and the have-nots. Glaring socioeconomic, racial, gender, special needs, and system-wide inequities in access to, use of, and support and achievement with quality technology in America's classrooms is evident across the country.[68]

Computers and Internet access are often portrayed as the great equalizers for impoverished children and youth. There is little doubt that effectively used technology can offer an influx of valuable, low-cost resources such as access to mentors, experts, remote scientific instruments, and current information in relevant classroom topics.[69] Yet in spite of these promises, there is a widening digital divide between the poor and the wealthy. For example, in 1999, there was a 35% gap in connected public school classrooms between schools serving the lowest and highest income brackets.[70] Teachers in low-income settings have less access to technical and instructional support than teachers in average- or high-socioeconomic settings. The Children's Partnership, a national policy and strategy center with a special interest in disadvantaged youth, reported that content issues for both low-income youth and their families are among the new dimensions of the digital divide because "academic success is tightly correlated to parental involvement and support of their children, capturing parents' interest and improving their technological literacy may directly translate into improved student academic success."[71] Specifically, the greater use of technology not only for entertainment and gaming but for more formal learning purposes can be approached by a greater emphasis on parental technology education.[72]

Unfortunately, because a disproportionate number of students from low-income backgrounds are African American, Hispanic, or Native American, students from these races or origin groups are also more frequently deprived of classroom-level access to technology, to quality technology learning opportunities, and to competent technical support in their schools. According to recent national surveys, these same minority students are much less likely than their largely middle class White counterparts to (a) have a computer at home, (b) have a parent who uses a computer at work, and (c) have access to the Internet.[73] The potential implications for K–12 students in terms of academic achievement are evident. If family and cultural influences greatly enhance and support the children's learning processes and shape the opportunities presented to them, then clearly more equitable technology use and access is desirable. Educators and school and community leaders can play an active role in pursuing comparable in-school and beyond-school access and use of technology across race and ethnic groups, not only for students but for their families as well.[74]

Distressing, too, is the recent data from the U.S. Department of Education showing the widening gap between students with disabilities and those without disabilities. Students with special needs (a) have lower school-completion rates, (b) are more likely to be unemployed, (c) experience higher arrest rates, and (d) are less likely to live independently as participants in their own communities.[75] Federal law mandates that schools accept responsibility for providing equal educational opportunities, known as *free appropriate public education*, to individuals with disabilities.[76] This is a responsibility that should be considered when schools acquire technology, and special educators should be well trained in making the necessary accommodations including assistive technologies. Recent studies have found that major barriers still exist throughout the K–12 public schools for special needs students in equitable access, use, and support for disabled-accessible technologies such as computers and other learning devices.[77]

Given the well-known gender differences in learning styles and preferences, it is not surprising that these same observed gender differences reflect themselves in the way that young girls choose (or do not choose) to interact with the new technologies. Girls are often turned off by traditional approaches to technology. Studies consistently demonstrate that girls believe they are as capable of using technology as boys; they just do not access it as often because they are not interested in it.[78] Based on these gender disparities in the differing rates of access and use of technology, researcher Turkle concluded that girls are not computer phobic, they are just computer reticent. Turkle stated, "Girls tend to see computers as tools, whereas they believe boys use them as toys, substituting computer skills for social skills. Girls' reluctance stems from an unwillingness to make that trade."[79] The American Association of University Women's Commission on Technology, Gender, and Teacher Education has developed a variety of recommendations for drawing more women and girls in to computer science and related technical fields and for making them generally more comfortable with the culture of technology.[80]

Activity

This activity is designed to assist you in evaluating the existing socioeconomic, gender, racial and ethnic, and special needs students' technology gaps that continue to exist in the homes, school, and immediate community surrounding your host school. The North Central Regional Educational Laboratory hosts "enGauge," a professional development program that has been designed to help school districts and individual schools plan and evaluate their system-wide use of educational technology.[81] This assignment has been adapted using their materials with particular emphasis on the digital divide analytic framework they devised. Using the chart in Fig. 4.6, survey your host school considering the equity indicators listed.[82]

Reflective Narrative

On the basis of your findings, write a(n) (imaginary) letter to the local school board summarizing your results and providing a list of specific recommended changes and improvements that you would like to suggest in terms of the access, use of, and support for technology for identified groups within your host school. Make sure that you provide some research support for the specific changes that you envision for your host school. (Hint: the enGauge site at the National Regional Education Laboratory Web site has a wealth of computer-linked research data on the questions contained in this chart. See http://www.ncrel.org/engauge/)

Directions: Respond appropriately to each of the following questions:
I. Indicators of Socioeconomic Digital Equity
1. Is there equitable school access to technology for all socioeconomic groups in the school? At the building level? At the classroom level? Speak with the media specialist at your school. Inquire about the student use of the school's computer and media facilities.
2. Is there equitable beyond-school access to technology for all socioeconomic groups in the home? In the local public (i.e., library access)? Speak with the librarian at your local library. Inquire about the student use of the library's computer facilities.
3. Equity does not necessarily mean equal. Students with socioeconomic status disadvantages may actually need additional resources to achieve equitable opportunity. Speak with school leaders. Are there any innovative programs being developed or grants being written to provide all students with laptop computers? Are there any innovative outreach programs to enhance the computer skills of the parents in the school?
4. Is there are Computer/Technology Club at your school? What is the gender, racial or ethnic, and socioeconomic status composition of the membership? Speak with the club's president. Share your findings and discuss them with the club president. If there are apparent inequities in representation, can you com up with some suggestions to ensure greater participation by all social groups in the school?
II. Indicators of Racial/Ethnic Digital Equity
5. Inquire from the central office of your school or local district whether any data has been collected locally on home and public-access use of computes by minority groups in the community.
6. Inquire from the central office of your school or local school district whether any data has been collected locally on the extent of computer ownership and use of computers by minority groups in the community. Do they have access to a full range of Internet services (i.e., email, World Wide Web, district intranet, etc.)? Inquire about the possibility of organizing a local focus group composed of minority parents to address issues of ownership, access, use, and support.
7. Inquire at local computer stores whether any special or bulk purchase programs or subsidized connectivity programs have been proposed in conjunction with local banks and community leaders to ensure greater minority computer ownership. If not, why?
III. Indicators of Gender Digital Equity
8. Observe and inquire whether girls are encouraged to participate in technology-oriented events and classes at the school.
9. Observer and inquire whether classroom games and educational software reflect the interests of girls.
10. Are the female teachers at the school adequately trained and comfortable with using technology and computer applications in all their everyday classroom teaching?

(continued)

11. Do the computer games and software that are available for student use equally accommodate different learning styles?
12. Is technology integrated into club activities that appeal to large numbers of female students (e.g., like the school Writing Club)?
13. Are female students being assisted in developing their own individual Web sites that can be personalized, updated, and continually reconstructed to reflect changing interests? Have female students been encouraged to discover some of the "girl talk" sites where they can conduct online discussions with other young girls of their own age in different countries and states? Speak with your school's media coordinator about the possibility of offering an afterschool workshop on these technologies.
III. Indicators of Special Needs Students' Digital Equity
14. With special needs students it is not always possible to take the students out into the community, but technology can bring the community to them. Does your school provide any opportunities for special needs students to videoconference with students from other schools on collaborative projects?
15. Special needs students themselves report a significant decline in their fear of stigmatization when communication is electronic (i.e., technology can help disabilities disappear for these students). What special opportunities have been provided at your host school to encourage special needs students to develop electronic friendship networks with students from other schools, states, and countries?
16. Do you observe that special needs students are using the computer largely for drills and repetitive learning activities while their nondisabled peers are encouraged to use the computer to develop more complex creatively diverse cognitive skills?
17. Do special needs students tend to work in isolation to complete their computer assignments while nondisabled students are provided more collaborative, problem-solving activities to complete?
18. Visit the local assistive technology center in your community. Inquire about its availability and use by the special needs students at your school. Have they purchased any disabled-accessible technology or software that might be appropriate for special needs students at your school?
19. Ask the special education teacher at your school about the technology needs of her special needs students.

FIG. 4.6.   Survey of digital age equity in American public schools.[83]

Related Readings

American Association of University Women (AAUW) Education Foundation—Commission on Technology, Gender, and Teacher Education. (1998). *Gender gaps: Where schools still fail our children.* Washington, DC: Author.

American Association of University Women (AAUW) Education Foundation—Commission on Technology, Gender, and Teacher Education. (1998). *Tech-savvy: Educating girls in the new computer age.* Washington, DC: Author.

The Children's Partnership. (2000). *Online content for low income and underserved Americans: The digital divide's new frontier.* Washington, DC: Author.

Heaviside, S., Rowland, C., Hurst, C., & McArthur, E. (2000, Spring). What are the barriers to the use of advanced telecommunications for students with disabilities in public schools? *Educational Statistics Quarterly, 2*(1), 1–2.

National Public Radio, the Kaiser Family Foundation, & the JFK School of Government at Harvard University. (February 2000). *National Survey of American Adults and Children on Technology/National Survey of American Kids on Technology.* Retrieved July 10, 2005, from http://www.npr.org/ programs/specials/poll/technology/ technology.kids.html

National Broadcast System. (1999, 2000). *Digital divide* (2-part PBS film series Web site). Retrieved July 10, 2005, from http://www.pbs.org/digitaldivide/index.html

Revenaugh, M. (2000). Beyond the digital divide: Pathways to equity. *Technology and Learning, 20*(10), 38–40, 44–49.

Silverman, S. (1998). *Guidance, gender equity, and technology education.* Hartford, CT: Vocational Equity Research, Technology, and Evaluation.

Warren-Sams, B. (1997). *Closing the equity gap in technology access and use.* Portland, OR: Center for Origin, Race, and Sex Equity (CNORSE), Northwest Regional Educational Laboratory and the Northwest Educational Technology Consortium.

Williams, C. (2000). *Statistics in brief: Internet access in U.S. public schools and classrooms, 1994–1999.* Washington, DC: National Center for Education Statistics.

NOTES

[1]Bobbitt, F. (1913). *The supervision of city schools: Some general principles of management applied to the problems of city school systems.* Twelfth Yearbook, Part I, National Society for the Study of Education. Bloomington, IN: Public School Publishing Company, p. 1.

[2]Ross, E. (1906). *Social control.* As cited in Karier, C. J., Violas, P., & Spring, J. (Eds.). (1972) *Roots of crisis: American education in the twentieth century.* Chicago: Rand McNally.

[3]Heilbroner, R. (1980), p. 175. As cited in Orr, D. W. (1992). *Ecological literacy: Education and the transition to a post-modern world.* Albany: State University of New York Press.

[4]de Chardin, T. (1965), pp. 43–44. As cited in Miller, J. (1993). *The holistic curriculum.* Toronto, Ontario, Canada: OISE Press, p. 76.

[5]Apple, M., & Beane, J. A. (Eds.). (1995). *Democratic schools.* Washington, DC: Association for Curriculum and Development; Smyth, J. (Ed.). (1993). *A socially critical view of the self-managed school.* Washington, DC: Falmer; David J. (1989). Synthesis of research on school based management. *Educational Leadership, 71*(1), 45–53; Karier, C. J. (1986). *The individual, society, and education: A history of American educational ideas* (2nd ed., pp. 286–362). Urbana: University of Illinois Press; Spring J. (1996). *American education* (7th ed.). New York: McGraw-Hill.

[6]Smyth, J. (1993). *A socially critical view of the self-managed school.* Washington, DC: Falmer, p. 3.

[7]Whitmyer, C. (Ed.). (1993). *In the company of others: Making community in the modern world.* New York: Jeremy P. Tarcher/Perigee Books, p. xx.

[8]Smyth, J. (Ed.). (1993). *A socially critical view of he self-managed school.* Washington, DC: Falmer, pp. 35–48 passim.

[9]McDaniel, T. R. (1989). Demilitarizing public education: School reform in the era of George Bush. *Phi Delta Kappan, 42*, 15–18.

[10]Shea, C. M., Kahane, E., & Sola, P. (Eds.). (1989). *The new servants of power: A critique of the 1980s educational reform movement.* Westport, CT: Greenwood, pp. 12–16, passim.

[11]Kozol, J. (1991). *Savage inequalities: Children in America's schools.* New York: Crown.

[12]Orr, D. W. (1992). *Ecological literacy: Education and the transition to a post-modern world.* Albany: State University of New York Press.

[13]Bowers, C. A. (1995). *Educating for an ecologically sustainable culture: Rethinking moral education, creativity, intelligence, and other modern orthodoxies.* Albany: State University of New York Press; Bowers, C. A. (1993). *Educational, cultural myths, and the ecological crisis: Toward deep changes.* Albany: State University of New York Press.

[14]Smith, G. A. (1992). *Education and the environment: Learning to live with limits.* Albany: State University of New York Press.

[15]Traina, F., & Darley-Hill, S. (Eds.). (1995). *Perspectives in bioregional education.* Troy, OH: North American Association for Environmental Education.

[16]Henderson, J. G., & Kesson, K. R. (1999). *Understanding democratic curriculum leadership.* New York: Teachers College Press.

[17]Esteva, G., & Prakash, M. S. (1998). *Grassroots post-modernism: Remaking the soil of cultures.* New York: ZED.

[18]Sobel, D. (2004). *Place-based education: Connecting classrooms and schools.* Barrington, MA: The Orion Society.

[19]Winters, W. G. (1993). *African American mothers and urban schools: The power of participation.* New York: Lexington.

[20]Cornbleth, C. (1990). *Curriculum in context* (pp. 120–121 passim). New York: Falmer; Spring, J. (1996). *American education* (7th ed.). New York: McGraw-Hill; Mercier, R. (1996). The greening of organizations. *Administration and Society, 27,* 459–472; Bolman, L. G., & Deal, T. E. (1992). *Reframing organizations: Artistry, choice, and leadership.* San Francisco: Jossey-Bass; Zeichner, K. (1991). Contradictions and tensions on the professionalization of teaching and the democratization of …. *Teachers College Record, 92,* 363–374; Sergiovanni, T., & Corbally, J. (Eds.). (1984). *Leadership and organizational culture.* Urbana: University of Illinois Press; Smith, G. A. (1994). Preparing teachers to restructure schools. *Journal of Teacher Education, 45,* 18–30; Smyth, J. (Ed.). (1993). *A socially critical view of the self-managed school.* Washington, DC: Falmer; Foster, W. P. (1986). *Paradigms and promises: New approaches to educational administration.* Buffalo, NY: Prometheus Books.

[21]This exercise has been inspired by some of the classroom assignments and discussions developed by Professors Fritz Mengert and Kathleen Casey, College of Education, University of North Carolina at Greensboro.

[22]Eckert, P. (1989). *Jocks and burnouts: Social categories and identity in high school.* New York: Teachers College Press; McLaren, P. (1989). *Life in schools: An introduction to critical pedagogy in the foundations of education.* New York: Longman; Van Berkun, D. W. (1995). The classroom with the empowered student. In M. Richardson, K. Lane, & J. Flanigan (Eds.), *School empowerment* (pp. 277–288). Lancaster, PA: Technomic Publishing Company.

[23]Van Berkum, D. W. (1995). The classroom with the empowered student. In M. Richardson, K. Lane, & J. Flanigan (Eds.), *School empowerment* (pp. 277–288). Lancaster, PA: Technomic Publishing Company.

[24]LaMorte, M. (1996). *School law: Cases and concepts* (pp. 84–188 passim). Boston: Allyn & Bacon.

[25]Sergiovanni, T. J. (1991). *Moral leadership: Getting to the heart of school improvement.* San Francisco, CA: Jossey-Bass; Shor, I. (1992). *Empowering education: Critical teaching for social change.* Chicago: University of Chicago Press; Smyth, J. (1991). *Teachers as collaborative learners: Challenging dominant forms of supervision.* Philadelphia: Open University Press.

[26]LaMorte, M. (1996). *School law: Cases and concepts* (pp. 189–283 passim). Boston: Allyn & Bacon.

[27]Hays, S. P. (1964, October). The politics of reform in municipal government in the Progressive era. *Pacific Northwest Quarterly, 55,* pp. 157–169; Russo, C. J. (1992). The legal status of school boards in the intergovernmental system. In P. First & H. Walberg (Eds.), *School boards:*

Changing local control (pp. 3–18). Berkeley, CA: McCutcheon; Spring, J. (1996). Local control, choice, charter schools, and privatization. *American Education* (7th ed., pp. 171–192). New York: McGraw-Hill.

[28]Institute for Educational Leadership. (1986). *School boards: Strengthening grass roots leadership*. Washington:, DC: Institute for Educational Leadership.

[29]Chart completely reconfigures that developed by Institute for Educational Leadership, *op cit*, p. 4.

[30]Spivak, H. S. (1973). *School decentralization and community control: Policy in search of a research agenda*. Boston: Institute for Responsive Education.

[31]Grant, C. (Ed.). (1979). *Community participation in education*. Boston: Allyn & Bacon; Medgley, C., & Woods, S. (1993). Beyond site-based management: Empowering teachers to reform schools. *Phi Delta Kappan, 75*, 245–252; Smith, G. (1994). Participating teachers to restructure schools. *Journal of Teacher Education, 45*, 18–30; Wood, G. (1986). Action for democratic education. *Issues in Education, 4*, 287–300.

[32]Katz, M. (1968). *The irony of early school reform*. Cambridge, MA: Harvard University Press.

[33]Comer, J. P. (1980). *Schoolpower: Implications of an intervention project*. New York: Free Press; Epstein, J. L. (1986, November). *Toward an integrated theory of family-school connections* (Rpt. No. 3). Baltimore: Center for Research on Elementary and Middle Schools; Fagnano, C. L., & Werber, B. Z. (Eds.). (1994). *School, family, and community interaction: A view from the firing lines*. Boulder, CO: Westview; Henderson, A. T. (1987). *The evidence continues to grow: Parent involvement improves education*. Columbia, MD: National Coalition of Citizens in Education; Herrick, S. C., & Epstein, J. L. (1991, August). *Improving school and family partnerships in urban elementary schools: Reading activity packets and school newsletters* (CDS Rpt. No. 19); Reglin, G. L. (1993). *At-risk "parent and family" involvement: Strategies for low income families of unmotivated and underachieving students.*

Springfield, IL: Thomas; Ryan, B. A., Adams, G. R., Gullotta, T. P., Weissberg, R., & Hampton, L. (Eds.). (1995). *The family–school connection: Theory. research. and practice*. Thousand Oaks, CA: Sage; Winters, W. C. (1993). *African American mothers and urban schools: The power of participation*. New York: Lexington.

[34]Henderson, A. As cited in Nieto, S. (1992), *Affirming diversity: The sociopolitical context of multicultural education*. New York: Lexington.

[35]Henderson, A., Marburger, C., & Ooms, T. (Eds.). (1986). *Beyond the bake sale: An educator's guide to working with parents*. Washington, DC: National Committee for Citizens in Education, pp. 85–90.

[36]Epstein, J. L. (1986, November). *Toward an integrated theory of family-school connections* (Rpt. No. 3). Baltimore: Center for Research on Elementary and Middle Schools.

[37]Comer, J. P. (1980). *Schoolpower: Implications of an intervention project*. New York: Free Press; Epstein, J. L. (1986, November). *Toward an integrated theory of family–school connections* (Rpt. No. 3). Baltimore: Center for Research on Elementary and Middle Schools; Epstein, J. L. & Dauber, S. L. (1989). *Teacher attitudes and practices of parent involvement in inner-city elementary and middle schools* (Rpt. No. 33). Baltimore: Center for Research on Elementary and Middle Schools, Johns Hopkins University; Fagnano, C. L., & Werber, B. Z. (Eds.). (1994). *School, family and community interaction: A view from the firing lines*. Boulder, CO: Westview; Henderson, A. T. (1987). *The evidence continues to grow: Parent involvement improves student achievement*. Columbia, MD: National Coalition of Citizens in Education; Reglin, G. L. (1993). *At-risk "parent and family" involvement: Strategies for low income families of unmotivated and underachieving students*. Springfield, IL: Thomas; Ryan, B. A., Adams, G. R., Gullotta, T. P., & Hampton, L. (Eds.). (1995). *The family– school connection: Theory, research, and practice*. Thousand Oaks, CA: Sage; Winters, W. C. (1993). *African American mothers and urban schools: The power of participation*. New York: Lexington.

[38]Herrick, S. C. & Epstein, J. L. (1991, August). *Improving school and family partnerships in urban elementary schools: Reading activity packets and school newsletters* (CDS Rpt. No. 19).

[39]Menacker, J., Hurwitz, E., & Weldom, W. (1988). As cited in C. L. Fagnano & B. Z. Werber (Eds.). (1994). *School, family, and community interaction: A view from the firing lines.* Boulder, CO: Westview.

[40]Henderson, A., Marburger, C., & Ooms, T. (Eds.). (1986). *Beyond the bake sale: An educator's guide to working with parents.* Washington, DC: National Committee for Citizens in Education, pp. 91–93.

[41]National Commission on Excellence in Education. (1983). *A nation at risk.* Washington, DC: U.S. Government Printing Office.

[42]Epstein, J. L. (1986, November). *Toward an integrated theory of family-school connections* (Rpt. No. 3). Baltimore: Center for Research on Elementary and Middle Schools.

[43]Martin, J. R. (1995). *The schoolhome: Rethinking schools for changing families.* Cambridge, MA: Harvard University Press.

[44]Commission on Work, Family, and Citizenship. (1988). *The forgotten half: Non-college youth in America. An interim report.* Washington, DC: William T. Grant Foundation; Johnston, W. B. & Packer, A. H. (1987). *Work force 2000: Work and workers in the 21st century.* Indianapolis, IN: Hudson Institute; Klerman, J., & Karoly, L. (1995). *The transition to stable employment: The experience of US youth in their early labor market career.* Berkeley, CA: Rand Institute/NCRVE; Law, C. J., Knuth, R. A., & Bergman, S. (1992). What does the research say about school-to-work transition? Oak Brook, IL: NCREL, WWW NCREL. Retrieved July 9, 2005, from http:www.ncrel.org/sdrs/areas/sfw_esps/%sch2wrk.htm homepage; National Center on Education and the Economy. (1990). *America's choice: High skills or low wages! The report of the commission on the skills of the America's laborforce.* Rochester, NY: Author; Stern, D., & Eichorn, D. (1989). *Adolescence and work: Influences on social structure, labor mar-*

kets, and culture. Hillsdale, NJ: Lawrence Erlbaum Associates.

[45]Stern, D., Finklestein, N., Stone, J., Latting, J., & Dornsife, C. (1995). *School to work: Research on programs in the United States.* Washington, DC: Falmer, p. 9.

[46]*Ibid.*

[47]Lakes, R. D. (Ed.). (1994). *Critical education and work: Multidisciplinary approaches.* Norwood, NJ: Ablex; Violas, P. (1978). *The training of the urban working class: A history of twentieth century American education.* Chicago: Rand McNally. The National Vocation Education (Smith–Hughes) Act of 1917, Pub.L. No.347, 64th Cong., Stat.703 (1917).

[48]Etizoni, A. (1993). The spirit of community: The reinvention of American society. New York: Simon & Schuster, p. 110.

[49]*Ibid.*

[50]Lakes, R. D. (Ed.). (1994). *Critical education and work: Multidisciplinary approaches.* Norwood, NJ: Ablex; Carl D. Perkins Vocational and Applied Technology Education Amendments of 1998, Pub.L. No. 105-332, 112 Stat. 3076 (October 31, 1998); Carl D. Perkins Vocational and Applied Technology Education Act of 1990, Pub.L. No. 101-392.

[51]This chart was suggested by information found in two sources: Law, C. J., Knuth, R. A., & Bergman, S. (1992). *What does the research say about school-to-work transition?* (pp. 12–13). Oak Brook, IL: NCREL, WWW, NCREL Web site homepage; and Lakes, R. (Ed.). (1994). *op cit* (p. 167).

[52]Lakes, R. D. (Ed.) (1994). *Critical education and work: Multidisciplinary approaches.* Norwood, NJ: Ablex.

[53]O'Hanlon, T. (1980, Spring). Interscholastic athletics, 1900–1940: Shaping citizens for unequal roles in the modern industrial state. *Educational Theory, 30*, 89–103.

[54]Spring, J. (1972). *Education and the rise of the corporate liberal state.* Boston: Beacon.

[55]Violas, P. (1978). *The training of the urban working class: A history of twentieth century American education.* Chicago: Rand McNally.

[56]Sedlak, M., Wheeler, C., Pullin, D., & Cusick, P. (1986). Student employment and extracurricular sports. In *Selling students short: Classroom bargains and academic reform in the American high school* (pp. 59–68). New York: Teachers College Press.

[57]Spring, J. (1972). *Education and the rise of the corporate liberal state*. Boston: Beacon.

[58]Larkin, R.W. (1979). *Suburban youth in cultural crisis*. New York: Oxford University Press.

[59]Stern, D. & Eichorn, D. (Eds.). (1989). *Adolescence and work: Influences on social structure, labor markets, and culture*. Hillsdale, NJ: Lawrence Erlbaum Associates.

[60]Lewin-Epstein, N. (1981). *Youth employment during high school: An analysis of high school and beyond: A national longitudinal study for the 80s*. Chicago: National Longitudinal Center for Educational Statistics; National Association of Secondary School Principals. (1984). *The mood of American youth*. Reston, VA: Author; Nieto, S. (1992). *Affirming diversity: The sociopolitical context of multicultural education*. New York: Longman; Sedlak, M., Wheeler, C., Pullin, D., & Cusick, P. (1986). Student employment and extracurricular sports. In *Selling students short: Classroom bargains and academic reform in the American high school* (pp. 59–68). New York: Teachers College Press.

[61]America and Gun Violence. Coalition to Stop Gun Violence. (2004), Fact Sheet: Gun Violence. Retrieved July 10, 2005 at http://www.csgv.org/new/ p. 1. [Reported at National Education Association, Health Information Network/School and Community Safety web site (April 14, 2005). Statistics: Gun violence in our communities. Retrieved July 10, 2005 from http://neahin.org/programs/schoolsafety/gunsafety/statistics.htm; Cook, P. J. & Ludwig, J. (May, 1997). *Guns in America: National Survey on Private Ownership and Use of Firearms*. Washington, DC: National Institute of Justice. p. 2. Retrieved July 10, 2005 from http:// www.ncjrs.org/txtfiles/165476.txt. Reported at National Education Association, Health Information Network/School and Community Safety web site (April 14,

2005). Statistics: Gun violence in our communities. p.1. Retrieved July 10, 2005 from http://neahin.org/programs/schoolsafety/gunsafety/statistics.htm; Children and Gun Violence. Center for Disease Control and Protection. Rates of homicide, suicide, and firearm-related death among children—26 industrialized nations. *Morbidity and Mortality Weekly Report, 46*(5), 101–105. Reported at National Education Association, Health Information Network/School and Community Safety web site (April 14, 2005). Statistics: Gun violence in our communities. p.1. Retrieved July 10, 2005 from http://neahin.org/programs/schoolsafety/ gunsafety/statistics.htm; Centers for Disease Control and Protection, National Center for Health Statistics.(2005). *Mortality data from the National Vital Statistics System for 2003*. Retrieved July 10, 2005 from http://www.cdc.gov/ nchs/about/major/dvs/mortdata.htm. Reported at Illinois Council against Handgun Violence. (February 28, 2005). *Kids and gun violence factsheet*, p. 1 Retrieved July 10, 2005, from http://www.ichv.org/kidsandguns.htm; American Schools, Children and School Violence. Department of Education and U.S. Department of Justice (November, 2004). *Indicators of School Crime and Safety: 2004*. Retrieved July 10, 2005, from http://nces.ed.gov/pubsearch/ pubsinfo.asp?pubid = 2005002. Reported at U.S. Department of Education. (November 29, 2004). Press release: Violent crime rate against students drops, new report says, pp.1–2. Retrieved July 10, 2005, from http://www.ed.gov/news/pressreleases/2004/11/11292004.html; Miller, M., Azrael, D., & Hemenway, D. (2002). Firearm availability and unintentional firearm deaths, suicide, and homicide among 5-14 year olds. *The Journal of Trauma, 52*(2), 267–275; Fingerhut, L. A., Christoffel, K. K. (Summer/Fall 2002). Firearm-related death and injury among children and adolescents. *The future of children, 12*(2), 32. Retrieved July 10, 2005, from http://www.futureofchildren.org/pubs-info2825/pubs-info_show.htm?doc_id= 154414; Schuster, M. A., Franke, T. M., Bastian, A. M., et al. (2000, April). Firearm storage patterns in U.S. homes with children. *American Journal of Public Health, 90*(4), 588–594; Sheley, J. F., & Wright, J. D. (1998, October). *High school youth, weapons, and violence: A national survey.* National Institute of Juvenile Justice Research in Brief. Washington, DC: National Institute of Juvenile Justice. Reported in Fingerhut, L. A., & Christoffel, K. K. (2002, Summer/Fall). Firearm-related death and injury among children and adolescents. *The future of children, 12*(2), 32. Retrieved July 10, 2005, from http://www.futureofchildren.org/pubs-info2825/pubs-how.htm?doc_id=154414; U.S. Department of Education. (October, 2000). *U.S. Department of Education Report on State Implementation of the Gun-Free Schools Act, School Year 1998–99,* p.2. Washington, DC: U.S. Department of Education. Reported at National Education Association, Health Information Network/School and Community Safety web site (April 14, 2005). *Statistics: Gun violence in our communities,* p.1. Retrieved July 10, 2005, from http://neahin.org/programs/schoolsafety/gunsafety/statistics.htm; Bullying and Hate-related Graffiti. Department of Education and U.S. Department of Justice (November, 2004). *Indicators of School Crime and Safety: 2004.* Retrieved July 10, 2005, from http://nces.ed.gov/pubsearch/pubsinfo.asp?pubid=2005002. Reported at U.S. Department of Education (November 29, 2004). Press release: Violent crime rate against students drops, new report says, pp.1–2. Retrieved July 10, 2005, from http://www.ed.gov/news/pressreleases/2004/11/11292004.html; Children and Media Violence. American Academy of Pediatrics. (2005). *Understanding the impact of media on children and teens,* p. 1. Retrieved July 10, 2005, from http://www.aap.org/family/mediaimpact.htm; Kaiser Family Foundation. (April, 2003). *Key facts: TV violence,* p.1. Retrieved July 10, 2005, from http://www.kff.org/entmedia/3335-index.cfm; National Center for Children Exposed to Violence. (June 14, 2005). *Media violence,* p. 1. Retrieved June 26, 2005 from http://www.nccev.org/violence/media.html; Lomonaco, C. (Fall, 2004). *Fact sheet: Media vi-*

olence. Riverside, CA: Southern California Center of Excellence on Youth Violence, p. 1. Retrieved July 10, 2005, from http://www.stopyouthviolence.ucr.edu/publications/factsheets/mediaviolence.pdf; U.S. Department of Education. (1994). *Strong families, strong schools: Building community partnerships for learning,* p. 1. Retrieved July 10, 2005, from http://www.edutopia.org/php/ resources.php?id=Item_200634. Reported at TV Turnoff Network (April 8, 2004). *Facts and figures about our TV habit,* p. 1. Retrieved July 10, 2005, from http://www.tvturnoff.org/ research.htm; TV Turnoff Network. (April 8, 2004). *Facts and figures about our TV habit,* p. 1. Retrieved July 10, 2005, from http://www.tvturnoff.org/research.htm

[62]Anderson, C. S. (1982). The search for school climate: A review of the research. *Review of Educational Research, 52,* 368–420; Brown, D. (1994). Youth violence: Causes and solutions. *Thrust for Educational Leadership, 24,* 10; Garcia, P. (1994). Creating a safe school climate. *Thrust for Educational Leadership, 24,* 22.

[63]Rifkin, J. (1995). *The end of work: The decline of the global labor force and the dawn of the post-market era.* New York: Putnam, p. 210.

[64]*Ibid.*

[65]National Institute of Education. (1978). *Violent schools—safe schools: The safe school study report to Congress. Volume I.* Washington, DC: Government Printing Office.

[66]National Institute of Education. (1978). *Violent schools—safe schools: The safe school study report to Congress. Volume I.* Washington, DC: Government Printing Office; Hill, M. S., & Hill, F. W. (1994). *Creating safe schools: What principals can do.* Thousand Oaks, CA: Corwin Press.

[67]As cited in C. Lewis (2003). Best practices and strategies for bridging the digital divide. In C. M. Shea & W. S. Thomson (Eds.), *Teachers' manual for North Carolina educators* (p. 416). New York: McGraw-Hill.

[68]Warren-Sams, B. (1997). *Closing the equity gap in technology access and use.* Portland, OR:

Center for Origin, Race, and Sex Equity, Northwest Regional Educational Laboratory and the Northwest Educational Technology Consortium. Retrieved July 10, 2005 at http://www.nwrel.org/cnorse/booklets/equitygap/Equity_gap.pdf; Williams, C. (February 2000). *Statistics in brief: Internet access in U.S. public schools and classrooms, 1994–1999.* Washington, DC: National Center for Education Statistics. Retrieved July 10, 2005 from http://nces.ed.gov/pubs2000/2000086.pdf; National Public Radio, the Kaiser Family Foundation, and the JFK School of Government at Harvard University. (February 2000). *National survey of American adults and children on technology/National survey of American kids on technology.* Retrieved July 10, 2005 from http://www.npr.org/programs/specials/poll/technology/technology.kids.html; National Broadcasting System. (1999, 2000). *Digital divide.*(2 Pt PBS film series web site). Retrieved July 10, 2005 at http://www.pbs.org/digitaldivide/index.html

[69]North Central Regional Educational Laboratory, Technology Education, enGauge Web site. *A framework for effective technology use, digital age equity.* Retrieved July 10, 2005, from http://www.ncrel.org/engauge/framewk/index.htm

[70] Williams, C. (2000). *Statistics in brief: Internet access in U.S. public schools and classrooms, 1991–1999.* Washington, DC: National Center for Education Statistics.

[71]The Children's Partnership. (2000). *Online content for low income and underserved Americans: The digital divide's new frontier.* Washington, DC: Author.

[72]*Ibid.*

[73]North Central Regional Educational Laboratory, Technology Education, enGauge Web site. *A framework for effective technology use, indicator: racial equity.* Retrieved July 10, 2005, from http://www.ncrel.org/engauge/framewk/equ/racial/equracin.htm

[74]The Children's Partnership. (2000). *Online content for low income and underserved Americans: The digital divide's new frontier.* Washing-

ton, DC: Author; Warren-Sams, B. (1997). *Closing the equity gap in technology access and use.* Portland, OR: Center for Origin, Race, and Sex Equity (CNORSE), Northwest Regional Educational Laboratory and the Northwest Educational Technology Consortium; Public Broadcast System. (2000). *Digital divide special report.* Retrieved July 10, 2005, from http://www.pbs.org/digitaldivide/index.html

[75]Warren-Sams, B. (1997). *Closing the equity gap in technology access and use.* Portland, OR: Center for Origin, Race, and Sex Equity (CNORSE), Northwest Regional Educational Laboratory and the Northwest Educational Technology Consortium; Revenaugh, M. (2000). Beyond the digital divide: Pathways to equity. *Technology and Learning, 20*(10), pp. 38–40, 44–49.

[76]Heaviside, S., Rowland, C., Hurst, C., & McArthur, E. (2000, Spring). What are the barriers to the use of advanced telecommunications for students with disabilities in public schools? *Educational Statistics Quarterly, 2*(1), 1–2.

[77]*Ibid.*

[78]Silverman, S. (1998). *Guidance, gender equity, and technology education.* Hartford, CT: Vocational Equity Research, Technology, and Evaluation; American Association of University Women (AAUW) Education Foundation—Commission on Technology, Gender, and Teacher Education. (1998). *Gender gaps: Where schools still fail our children.* Washington, DC: Author; American Association of University Women (AAUW) Education Foundation—Commission on Technology, Gender, and Teacher Education. (1998). *Tech-savvy: Educating girls in the new computer age.* Washington, DC: Author.

[79]Turkle, S. (1995). *Life on the screen: Identity in the age of the internet.* New York: Simon & Schuster.

[80]American Association of University Women (AAUW) Education Foundation—Commission on Technology, Gender, and Teacher Education. (1998). *Gender gaps: Where schools still fail our children.* Washington, DC: Author; American Association of University Women (AAUW) Edu-

cation Foundation—Commission on Technology, Gender, and Teacher Education. (1998). *Tech-savvy: Educating girls in the new computer age.* Washington, DC: Author.

[81]North Central Regional Educational Laboratory, Technology Education, enGauge Web site. *A framework for effective technology use, indicator: Gender equity.* Retrieved July 10, 2005, from http://www.ncrel.org/engauge/framewk/equ/gender/equgenin.htm

[82]This chart was developed from the outstanding digital divide equity materials developed as part of the enGauge program hosted by the North Central Regional Educational Laboratory, Technology Education, enGauge Web site. Retrieved July 10, 2005, from http://www.ncrel.org/engauge/framewk index.htm

[83]*Ibid.* Reprinted by permission.

Section 5

No Child Left Untested

INTRODUCTION

In many ways, public education in the United States can be said to have begun as a social reform movement.[1] During the Industrial Revolution, cities in the Northeast became home to thousands of immigrants from many different countries who spoke many different languages. Out of concern that these "new Americans" would attempt to maintain the language and traditions of their homelands, many political and religious leaders joined the push for common schools. These social reformers argued that civil unrest could be managed by establishing common experiences between diverse groups through school attendance.[2]

This specter of responsibility to reform broader social conditions has contributed to the continual cycle of reform that haunts the field of education even today.[3] We are currently operating in a reform movement that has its roots in the 1983 publication of *A Nation at Risk*. This government report commissioned under President Ronald Reagan made this startling claim:

> If an unfriendly power had attempted to impose on America the mediocre educational performance that exists today, we might well have viewed it as an act of war. As it stands, we have allowed this to happen to ourselves. We have even squandered the gains in achievement made in the wake of the Sputnik challenge. Moreover, we have dismantled essential support systems which helped make those gains possible. We have, in effect, been committing an act of unthinking, unilateral educational disarmament.[4]

The writers of the report cited high rates of illiteracy; loss of intellectual moral and spiritual strength; declining scores on standardized achievement tests in science, math, and English; increasing percentages of remedial math courses in colleges and universities; and complaints from the military and business sectors of the high costs of "remedial education and training programs in such basic skills as reading, writing, spelling, and computation."[5] The report also noted that "on 19 academic tests American students were never first or second and, in comparison with other industrialized nations, were last seven times."[6] Further, these insufficiencies were contextualized within a changing economy that was increasingly demanding greater scientific and technological proficiency.

The report made five recommendations to remedy these perceived problems:

- *All students seeking a [high school] diploma be required to lay the foundations in the Five New Basics by taking the following curriculum during their 4 years of high school: (a) 4 years of English; (b) 3 years of mathematics; (c) 3 years of science; (d) 3 years of social studies; and (e) one-half year of computer science.*
- *Schools, colleges, and universities adopt more rigorous and measurable standards, and higher expectations, for academic performance and student conduct, and that 4-year colleges and universities raise their requirements for admission.*
- *Significantly more time be devoted to learning the New Basics. This will require more effective use of the existing school day, a longer school day, or a lengthened school year.*

- *Improve the preparation of teachers or to make teaching a more rewarding and respected profession.*
- *Citizens across the Nation hold educators and elected officials responsible for providing the leadership necessary to achieve these reforms, and that citizens provide the fiscal support and stability required to bring about the reforms we propose.*[7]

The alarming tone of this report established a sense of urgency and "accountability" that has pervaded educational reforms since the early 1980s. The concept of establishing national standards as the way to set benchmarks was deeply embedded in this report, and the utilization of standardized tests to assess the achievement of these benchmarks became equated with accountability. These two concepts, national standards and accountability, became the driving forces behind educational reform.

The most recent reform package, No Child Left Behind (NCLB) Act of 2001,[8] passed by a bipartisan effort in 2002, is the culmination of a progression of standards movements begun in 1983 and continued in both George Bush Sr.'s America 2000 and Clinton's Goals 2000. The legislation, approved quietly with little fanfare and little press, was signed in January 2002, just 4 months after the September 11th national tragedy. According to the United States Department of Education Web site,

> The Act is the most sweeping reform of the Elementary and Secondary Education Act (ESEA) since ESEA was enacted in 1965. It redefines the federal role in K–12 education and will help close the achievement gap between disadvantaged and minority students with their peers. It is based on four principles: stronger accountability for results, increased flexibility and local control, expanded options for parents, and an emphasis on teaching methods that have been proven to work.[9]

However, the implications of this reform have been monumental for states and school districts throughout the country. Combining both conservative and liberal ideologies, NCLB requires all schools to implement yearly assessments of all students in Grades 3 through 8 to determine their proficiency in math and reading. Yearly report cards indicate how well students are performing, and the data must be disaggregated by race, gender, socioeconomic status, and disability. Any school accepting Title I money must demonstrate adequate yearly progress (AYP). If a school fails to meet proficiency standards, it is deemed a school "in need of improvement." If certain subgroups of the student population (e.g., English language learners) do not perform well, then schools can also be labeled in need of improvement. Schools failing to demonstrate AYP for 2 years become labeled a low-performing schools. Students in low-performing schools may transfer to another public school in the district or a neighboring district if that school system agrees to accept them. If the school continues to fail to meet AYP for 5 years, "the school district must initiate plans for *restructuring* the school. This may include reopening the school as a charter school, replacing all or most of the school staff or turning over school operations either to the state or to a private company with a demonstrated record of effectiveness."[10]

NCLB also mandates that states ensure that every teacher in a core subject area meets the definition of "highly qualified." According to NCLB, highly qualified teachers have earned at least a bachelor's degree from a 4-year institution, are state certified, and are competent in at least one subject area. If a classroom lacks a highly qualified teacher, then the school district must notify the parents of these students. Further, states must demonstrate that they are making sincere efforts to ensure that highly qualified teachers staff classrooms in high-poverty and minority schools. However, critics have pointed out that to date, NCLB has not held states accountable for the continued lack of qualified teachers of poor and minority students, the supposed beneficiaries of the NCLB legislation.

Some lesser known components of the legislation require all high schools to report the names of their graduating seniors to the military, and school districts must certify to the state that their district has no policies denying students the right to participate in "constitutionally protected" prayers. The intent of this provision, according to then U.S. Education Secretary Rod Paige, was "to clarify the extent to which prayer in schools in legally protected."[11]

Although NCLB passed with little fanfare and with bipartisan support, the legislation has since been sorely criticized, and some school districts have refused to comply with the legislation, thus forfeiting their share (if any) of Title I money. President Bush, in his second term, declared his intent to extend NCLB to secondary education as well. One of the major criticisms is that there are insufficient funds to implement the required changes. Other critics suggest that NCLB is punitive, particularly to schools that serve low-income and minority students. Others have suggested that schools are being called on to fix social problems that are structural in nature. Many liberals argue that the legislation will eventually lead to the demise of public education. They contend that conservatives used NCLB as a way to hijack progressive ideals of equality and social justice while deceptively promoting vouchers and the privatization of public education.

The activities in this section provide an opportunity for you to think through some of the terms and catch phrases associated with the NCLB legislation. What kinds of resources and educational changes would be needed to create a public education system in which the needs of all children were met? Can all children attain even a basic educational foundation? How low of an achievement standard would be required to really establish a foundation that all children can attain? Think about children with severe mental and physical impairments. Do we, as a nation, really want to set a basement for everyone? Even if we did establish such a foundation, how would we know when it was met? Currently, the term *accountability* is treated solely as if it means scores on standardized tests. Rather than leaving

no child behind, we maintain that this "leaves no child untested." Further, we are skeptical that this testing regime bears any relation to the kind of accountability needed in our schools. Should schools be held accountable in other ways that lead to more socially just, healthy environments?

In this section, we provide some activities to help you reflect on these and related ideas. The first activity, Best Practice, considers the so-called practical assistance that is claimed to be offered by those touting research-based answers to educational questions. The next activity examines the criteria of Highly Qualified Teachers. How will states meet the demand for a highly qualified teacher in every classroom by the end of the 2005 to 2006 school year? The activity provides you an opportunity to ask teachers and principals about how this requirement has changed the way they conduct their professional lives. The English Language Learners, Immigrant, and Migrant Students in the Schools activity looks at some of the often overlooked subgroups within the schools. Children whose first language it not English face the prospect of teachers who do not speak their home language. Also, a sizable minority of children live migratory lives. They move seasonally with their parents planting and harvesting crops. Many of these children are absent for substantial portions of each school year. NCLB may help bring the needs of these children into focus, but does it provide resources to meet these needs? This activity helps you look at the resources available for these children. The No Child Left Untested activity takes a closer look at the impact of the requirements for standardized tests as a measure of accountability for the schools, teachers, and principals. This activity will guide you through interviews with principals, teachers, and others whose daily lives are tinted with a continual awareness that they will be judged successful or unsuccessful largely on the basis of a standardized test.

Recently, scholars have recommended that teachers learn ways to be sensitive to cultural differences while maintaining high standards. This research literature has recommended "other mothering," "warm demanding," and "colortalk" be included among a teacher's strategies for interpersonal interactions with students. This activity introduces you to these concepts and encourages you to learn more about how your styles of interacting with students may support or inhibit student learning. The final activity in this section is Healthy Bodies and Healthy Minds. As schools cut physical education classes and recess to devote more time to meeting national standards, what impact does this have on the health of students? This activity guides you through a brief investigation of how the health of our nation's children is put in jeopardy every day as a result of school practices and policies.

The activities included in this section do not exhaust the possibilities of exploration and investigation of the NCLB Act. Rather, they constitute a wide array of introductory activities intended to encourage you to question, critique, and think through political rhetoric and the ways it impacts the daily lives of children, parents, teachers, principals, and all others associated with the schools. Certainly, no one would argue with the desire to leave no child behind. How-

ever, teachers must question, critique, and actively think through the real-life impact of empty political slogans and promises. We all do want highly qualified teachers in the profession. Additionally, we want these highly qualified teachers to also be good teachers, and, we want these highly qualified, good teachers to meet the educational needs of all students in the schools. For this to be more than empty political rhetoric, all the people invested in schools need to provide resources (financial, intellectual, and emotional) necessary to accomplish this task.

Related Readings

Berube, M. R. (1994). *American school reform: Progressive, equity and excellence movements, 1883–1993*. New York: Praeger.

Darling-Hammond, L., French, L., & Garcia Lopez, S. P. (Eds.). (2002). *Learning to teach for social justice*. New York: Teachers College Press.

Spring, J. (2003). *The American school, 1642–2004* (6th ed.). New York: McGraw-Hill.

Zemelman, S., Daniels, H., & Hyde, A. (1998). *Best practice: New standards for teaching and learning in America's schools*. Portsmouth, NH: Heinemann.

BEST PRACTICES

Background

The idea behind the phrase best practices is that schools (and other social institutions) need to take a close look at what conclusions can be drawn from years of research to implement these into the daily routines of classrooms. Rather than following fads, the notion of best practices encourages teachers, principals, and other school personnel to stick with the "tried and true."

The NCLB legislation emphasizes the importance of teachers implementing best practices in their classrooms. To assist teachers in implementing best practices in their classrooms, the federal government provides a tool kit (http://www.ed.gov/teachers/nclbguide/nclb-teachers-toolkit.pdf) for teachers.

Activity

1. Examine the "Teachers Toolkit" carefully. What teaching strategies are recommended? What tools does the kit provide for teachers?

2. Interview a teacher at your host school. Has she seen this tool kit? Has she found it helpful in her teaching? Why or why not? What teaching strategies are in her personal tool kit for teaching? What does this teacher at your host school believe to be her secrets for success in teaching? Are these beliefs grounded in the research of best practices?

Reflective Narrative

Now that you have looked at the tool kit and talked with at least one teacher, think again about the idea of best practices. Do you think there can be "one best system" that can be identified and that will work for all children and all teachers in all schools? Do best practices differ according to the race, social class, or ability of your students?

Related Readings

Tyack, D. (1974). *The one best system: A history of American urban education*. Cambridge, MA: Harvard University Press.

Wong, H., & Wong, R. (1998). *The first days of school*. Mountain View, CA: Harry K. Wong Publications, Inc.

Zemelman, S., Daniels, H., & Hyde, A. (1998). *Best practice: New standards for teaching and learning in America's schools*. Portsmouth, NH: Heinemann.

HIGHLY QUALIFIED TEACHERS

Background

The Elementary Secondary Education Act, better known now as the NCLB Act, requires a highly qualified teacher for every classroom in the United States by the end of the 2005 to 2006 school year. How does the NCLB Act define highly qualified?

Highly Qualified Teachers. To be deemed highly qualified, teachers must (a) have a bachelor's degree, (b) have full state certification or licensure, and (c) prove that they know each subject they teach.[12]

Another provision of the NCLB Act is that parents must be notified if their child has been taught for four or more consecutive weeks by a teacher who does not meet the highly qualified criteria. States have implemented different procedures for determining highly qualified. Some states administer the Praxis II exam; others have dictated the kinds of college courses preservice teachers must take. Many rural areas are struggling to find highly qualified teachers in every subject, resulting in a 2004 amendment to NCLB that allows some flexibility for teachers in rural communities and for science teachers in meeting the highly qualified mandate.

Activity

1. Interview the principal of your host school. Ask about how the highly qualified teacher requirements have impacted the school. How have teachers been able to meet the highly qualified mandate? What percentage of the teachers at your host school met the highly qualified criteria before the NCLB legislation was passed? What percentage of the teachers meet this qualification now? Were some teachers shifted in their teaching assignments to better match the highly qualified criteria? (If so, find out who these teachers are if you can.) How has the teaching staff changed since the implementation of NCLB? Are there more or fewer teachers of color? Do more teachers have advanced degrees? Are there more or less teachers who have entered the teaching profession through alternative routes on staff now? If you are at a school that does not have highly qualified teachers in every classroom, ask the principal if parents have been informed. What was their response?

2. Interview a veteran teacher who has been impacted by the highly qualified criteria. This could be a teacher whose teaching area has been shifted to match the highly qualified criteria, or who was required to take additional coursework and staff development workshops, or who was required to take a standardized test such as Praxis II. Ask him or her the same questions that you asked the principal. Does she or he feel more highly qualified than before. Why or why not?

Reflective Narrative

Has your host school met the requirements of NCLB regarding having highly qualified teachers in every classroom? Did the flexibility written into the legislation work to the benefit of your host school? Why or why not? Investigate the loopholes in the legislation. In your view, is there a highly qualified teacher in every classroom in your host school? Why or why not? Now that you have investigated this issue more closely, what does highly qualified mean to you?

Related Readings

Cochran-Smith, M. (2002). Reporting on teacher quality: The politics of politics. *Journal of Teacher Education, 53,* 379–382.

Darling-Hammond, L., & Youngs, P. (2002). Defining "highly qualified teachers": What does "scientifically-based research" actually tell us? *Educational Researcher, 31*(9), 13–25.

Futrell, M. H. (1999). The Challenge of the 21st century: Developing a highly qualified cadre of teachers to teach our nation's diverse student population. *Journal of Negro Education, 68,* 318–334.

Oakes, J. (2001). The governor's teacher scholar initiative: Can The University of California bring highly qualified teaching to the state's poorest children? *Teacher Education Quarterly, 28,* 57–69.

ENGLISH LANGUAGE LEARNERS (ELLS), IMMIGRANT, AND MIGRANT STUDENTS IN SCHOOLS

Background

As the name of the NCLB Act implies, no children should be left out of the equation when school faculty and staff develop and implement curriculum and extracurricular activities. Yet clearly, some children are forgotten in the rush to create and meet new academic standards. Among those most often overlooked (intentionally or otherwise) are those students whose first or home language is not English.[13] Some children who speak Spanish, Chinese, Russian, or another language at home do not struggle in school. However, the academic progress of many other children is noticeably impeded by their lack of proficiency in English. Such students are labeled as English Language Learners (ELLs, or sometimes as Limited English Proficient students).

Most ELLs are the children of immigrants to the United States, children of families who came to our nation within the last couple generations. While struggling to find their place within a new culture and society, these children face the enormous challenge of learning English, a relatively large and complex language. In addition, they must face the dilemma of whether and/or how to maintain their home language and culture in a society that is frequently hostile to immigrants and their heritages. Many times the pressure to acculturate and assimilate to the dominant English-speaking norms cause ELLs to become disconnected from their home language and culture and lose the ability to communicate with their own parents, grandparents. or other family members. As they gain English language proficiency, these children frequently and prematurely face adult pressures and responsibilities as they are called on to translate for their family in financial, medical, or personal interactions. These responsibilities often compete with their education and the time they need to attend school or simply complete homework. The maturity and "fund of knowledge"[14] developed by these students in these interactions are not acknowledged or valued by most schools and most certainly not by the standardized exams required by the NCLB Act.

Additionally, many ELL students are the children of migrant farmworking families, families that move from state to state three, five, even seven times a year in search of work planting and harvesting the vegetables and fruits we all eat. These families earn below-poverty-level wages and generally live in substandard housing and without access to reasonable medical care. Although there are many native-born, English-speaking migrant families in the United States, the majority of our nation's migrant farm laborers are of Mexican heritage, and many of them are first and second-generation immigrants from Mexico. Thus, children in these families face the quadrupled challenges of language, culture, poverty, and constant movement. It should be no surprise that migrant students have the highest dropout rate of any subgroup in our schools.

Activity[15]

1. Ask your host teacher or principal about the resources available in your host school and district to accommodate the needs of ELL and migrant students. Look on the Internet for a "school report card" showing the sociocultural characteristics of students and teachers at your host school. Does the data you found on the Internet about your school match what you see with your own eyes when you are in the school?

2. Interview an administrator or counselor or ask for a "fact sheet" showing the cultural, ethnic, and linguistic backgrounds of the students, teachers, paraprofessionals, administrators, and custodial staff at your host school. How many different languages are spoken by the children and adults at your host school? Is the percentage of ELL students matched by an equal percentage of bilingual staff who speak the students' home languages? Is bilingual or bicultural education available or supported? Do any of the teachers have their classrooms labeled in more than one language? Do any teachers ever use the students' home language(s) during instruction? How many ESOL teachers are there in the school or district? What is the ratio of ESOL teachers to ELL students in the school and district? Are students served by "pull out" programs, or are their needs supposedly met within the regular education classroom? How are the ELLs and migrant kids doing in your host school and district? Is disaggregated data available to show how these kids are progressing in school?

Reflective Narrative

What can schools do when there isn't a match between the language spoken by the teachers and the language spoken by some of the students? What is working to benefit ELLs in your host school? What is not working?

As schools are increasingly challenged to meet AYP, the temptation to find ways to exclude ELL and migrant children from the assessment mea- sures increases. Many schools have tried to peti- tion for exemptions from testing for the ELLs. In the case of migrant children, many schools feel unduly judged by factors that are beyond their control. Which school should be held account- able for the education of a student who spends 6 to 8 weeks in each locale? In an effort to avoid re- sponsibility for these children, some schools and districts manage the testing cycle to avoid times when migrant students are in their schools. Is the testing cycle in your host school or district sched- uled around the migrant cycle? Is your host school in an urban, suburban, or rural location? Consider how ELL issues might be handled dif- ferently based on location. For example, rural school districts may be dramatically impacted by seasonal migration of migrant families with ELL children. There may be times when there are al- most no ELL children in the school and other times when as many as 25% or more of the stu- dent population may be ELLs. How is this cycle planned for and accommodated? What resources might a suburban or urban school have that a ru- ral school might not? Conversely, what resources might a rural school have that a suburban or urban school might not?

Related Readings

Igoa, C. (1995). *The inner world of the immigrant child*. New York: St. Martin's Press.

Lightbown, P., & Spada, N. (1999). *How languages are learned* (rev. ed.). New York: Oxford Univer- sity Press.

Power, B. M., & Hubbard, R. S. (1996). *Language de- velopment: A reader for teachers*. Englewood Cliffs, NJ: Merrill/Prentice Hall.

Valdes, G. (2001). *Learning and not learning English*. New York: Teachers College Press.

Salinas, C., & Fránquiz, M. (Eds.). (2004). *Field of hope: Educating migrant children for the future*. Charleston, WV: Clearinghouse on Rural Educa- tion and Small Schools.

Wortham, S., Murillo, E., Jr., & Hamann, E. (Vol. Eds.). (2001). *Education in the new Latino dias- pora: Policy and the politics of identity*. In B. Levinson & M. Gibson (Series Eds.), *Sociocultural studies of educational policy formation and appro- priation* (Vol. 2). Westport, CT: Ablex.

Name _____	Course/Section _____
Observation Site _____	Subject _____
Date _____ Other Information _____	

NO CHILD LEFT UNTESTED

Background

Because schools are under pressure from NCLB to meet AYP each year or face restructuring, the importance of performing well on standardized tests has become a matter of concern for the entire school. Principals are sometimes hired and fired on the basis of the results of this exam. Merit pay for teachers is often linked to exam results. Further, results of these standardized exams are even used to determine real estate values as some home buyers seek housing in districts with "good schools." With the stakes of testing increasing in these ways, many schools and districts have implemented programs intended to raise test scores for students.

Activity

1. Interview your host teacher about the test-taking strategies and preparation activities that have been implemented.[16] At the early elementary level, these strategies may include lessons on "bubbling in" rather than content per se. Ask your teacher to name all the aspects of schooling that have been impacted by the increasing importance of standardized tests. What tests are used at your host school? Are they norm-referenced or criterion-referenced tests? Does that make a difference? Why or why not?

2. Much of the testing is coordinated by the school's counselor, but sometimes schools or districts hire personnel whose sole responsibility is managing all aspects of standardized testing. Find out if your school or school district has a person responsible for test management. If so, interview that person using the preceding questions.

3. At the secondary level, special classes during the day or on weekends may be offered to help students pass graduation or exit exams. Schedule an observation of one of these classes. What strategies are being used to help students pass the exam? Note the racial and gendered makeup of the class. Talk to the students, if possible, about their experiences taking this kind of class and taking graduation exams.

Reflective Narrative

A generation ago, standardized testing was used for assessment of individual student achievement or placement in special education/gifted classes. Now, standardized tests administered to students are used to assess the achievement of teachers, principals, and whole schools as well as students. Is this a fair or even acceptable extension of the purpose of these exams?

In some places, grade-level promotion or graduation is tied to a standardized test. Students may receive passing grades but may not be promoted to the next grade or may not receive a diploma if they fail the related standardized test. Knowledge of the high stakes of these tests may place undue pressure on students and generate or increase test anxiety. Consider the feelings of a third grader who knows they will not go to fourth grade with their friends if they fail this exam.

Research and the experience of teachers has shown a close link between socioeconomic status of students and scores on standardized tests. If AYP is based on standardized tests, then might NCLB be punishing schools for the socioeconomic status of their parent population?

With such high stakes pinned to the tests, teachers and principals are tempted to cheat. For example, one study found 63 preservice teachers were asked to respond to the idea of cheating while administering a standardized test to their students. Over half said they would cheat under certain conditions such as benefit to the students or if the test was inappropriate. Cheating considered acceptable included giving hints, rewording items, and teaching to the exact test.[17] Does cheating on high-stakes tests constitute a threat to our moral character?

Related Readings

Erb, T. (2000). A responsive curriculum for ethically and pedagogically superior results. The editor reflects. *Middle School Journal, 32*(1), 4.

Gustafson, J. P. (2002). Missing the mark for low SES students. *Kappa Delta Pi Record, 38*, 60–63.

Popham, J. (2000). The score-boosting game. *American School Board Journal, 187*(6), 36–39.

Wellhousen, K., & Martin, N. K. (1995). Preservice teachers and standardized test administration: Their behavioral predictions regarding cheating. *Research in the Schools, 2*, 47–49.

"OTHER MOTHERING" AND "COLORTALK": MEETING THE NEEDS OF DIVERSE STUDENTS

Background

Census data shows that the United States as a whole is becoming more diverse. In 1990, the census showed 75.6% of the population was White; that percent dropped to 69.1% in 2000 and is predicted to drop to 50.1% by the year 2050[18] (http://www.censusscope.org). Meanwhile, the teaching force remains overwhelmingly White. According to a recent CBS news report, 90% of school teachers are White and 40% of schools have no minority teacher on staff (http://www.cbsnews.com/stories/2004/11/09/national/main654503.shtml).

Recently, scholars have turned attention toward positive factors related to culturally diverse students in schools. These scholars have identified culturally relevant or culturally sensitive educational practices as enhancing the achievement of students in schools. They have recommended that curriculum and pedagogy be adjusted for greater relevancy and sensitivity to the needs and cultural backgrounds of students in schools, especially those who differ culturally from the teachers and administrators.

These scholars have also written about warm demanding or other mothering responses of teachers in schools.[19] They have noted that some teachers respond to student needs, misbehaviors, and other difficulties in school in ways that reflect an understanding of the challenges faced by the student coupled with a demand that the student meet the academic and social requirements of the school setting. For example, if a student is sleeping in class, a teacher may acknowledge the students' need to work after school hours to help support her family while also reminding the student that more lucrative careers are available to high school and college graduates than to dropouts. Warm demanding or other mothering responses reflect the kind of cultural relevancy and sensitivity that recent scholars seek to encourage in classrooms.

Color talk is another culturally relevant and sensitive response that these scholars have encouraged from teachers in the schools. Rather than pretending to "not see color" or claiming that "all my students may as well be purple or green," these scholars have recommended that teachers acknowledge and talk about the ways in which some students are different from others. This may be as simple as a conversation about various hair styles and textures or as complicated as recognizing the legitimacy and importance of the use of nonstandard English in informal social contexts.

In efforts to leave no child behind, teachers must work on developing culturally relevant and culturally sensitive pedagogy including other mothering and warm demanding responses to students and the inclusion rather than exclusion of color talk.

Activity[20]

1. As you observe in the classroom, make note of the interactions between the teacher and stu-

149

dents. In particular, note any comments related to behavior, cultural background of the students or teacher, or the general importance of the subject matter being discussed. Describe the reactions of the teacher and students. Did any of these interactions include other mothering, warm demanding, or color talk? Ask the teacher what strategies he or she uses to incorporate the students' culture into their curriculum.

Reflective Narrative

Teacher A says that when she looks at her students, she does not see color; all she sees are students. Teacher B says that when she sees her students, she sees African American students, Hispanic students, male students, Asian female students, and so forth. What teacher do you think would be the most effective in the classroom? Why? What are the dangers of a "color blind" approach to teaching? Are there dangers of seeing color in the classroom? How might the exchanges you noted in your host classroom been modified to provide more support and show understanding of the student's cultural background while demanding academic achievement?

Related Readings

Collier, M. D. (2002). Changing the face of teaching: Preparing educators for diverse settings. *Teacher Education Quarterly, 29*, 49–59.

Irvin, J. J. (1990). *Black students and school failure: Policies, practices, prescriptions.* New York: Greenwood.

Irvine, J. J., & Armento, B. J. (2001). *Culturally responsive teaching: Lesson planning for elementary and middle grades.* New York: McGraw-Hill.

Ladson-Billings, G. (2003). *Critical race theory perspectives on the social studies: The profession, policies, and curriculum.* Greenwich, CT: Information Age Publishing.

Ladson-Billings, G. (2001). *Crossing over to Canaan: The journey of new teachers in diverse classrooms.* San Francisco: Jossey-Bass.

Ladson-Billings, G. (1994). *Dreamkeepers: Successful teaching of African-American children.* San Francisco: Jossey-Bass.

Thompson, A. (1998). Not for the color purple: Black feminist lessons for educational caring. *Harvard Educational Review, 68*, 522–554.

HEALTHY BODIES AND HEALTHY MINDS

Background

In 1946, President Harry Truman signed into law the National School Lunch Act (NSLA).[21] Faced with returning World War II soldiers who were malnourished, the NSLA was viewed as a "measure of national security to safeguard the health and well-being of the nation's children." Under NSLA guidelines, every school child would be guaranteed to receive an inexpensive, healthy meal at least once a day. In 1966, Congress supplemented the NSLA by enacting the Child Nutrition Act that established, among other things, a school breakfast program. Both Acts were premised on the belief that a healthy, well-nourished body would enhance learning and development. However, many would argue that it would be hard to find that inexpensive, nutritious school lunch in most school cafeterias. With the introduction of fast food vendors (e.g., Pizza Hut®, Taco Bell®) selling their wares in the cafeteria and school cafeterias trying to compete with these vendors by offering their own a la carte options (e.g., french fries), schools have veered far away from the central premise that healthy eating promotes healthy learning and development.

Childhood obesity has become a national public health concern, and many policymakers have begun looking at schools and the role they play in this national epidemic. Should schools be held accountable for the increasing number of overweight children? School districts throughout the United States have dropped physical education from their list of required courses students must take. Most high schools eliminated recess decades ago, but now, many elementary schools have eliminated recess to allow more time for teachers to cover math and reading. School lunches fall far short of meeting basic healthy dietary plans—with the most famous instance being President Reagan allowing ketchup to count as a "vegetable." Should schools be held accountable for not serving lunches that meet federal nutritional guidelines?

Activity

1. Spend some time in the school cafeteria of your host school. Record the food choices students are offered. If you can, obtain a lunch and/or breakfast menu for a month. Are outside vendors allowed? What beverages are offered? Compare these food choices to the recommended food guide pyramid (Fig. 5.1).

2. Eat lunch with a group of students in the cafeteria. Record what each student had on his or her plate. How does it compare with the pyramid?

3. Make a brief list of the different cultural groups represented in your host school and consider the menus from the perspective of these various groups. In what ways does the lunch or breakfast menu reflect various cultures? Does it reflect all of the various cultural groups in the school?

4. Interview the person in charge of the food services at your school. Find out what factors in-

fluence her choice of foods to serve. Ask her to respond to the criticism that schools are partially responsible for the increase of obesity in today's children.

5. Observe a physical education class. Ask the teacher how frequently students have physical education. How many students are in the class? In what kinds of activities are students participating? Are all students participating? Are the activities geared toward the athletically inclined male student or are activities varied to entice all students to participate? What happens to students who do not participate? Make note of the kind of equipment available for students. Are there adequate resources available so that all students can participate?

Reflective Narrative

On a scale ranging from 1 *(unhealthy)* to 10 *(very healthy)*, how healthy are the meals at your school? What does this reflect about your

school's commitment to the education of the whole child?

Think about the school breakfast and lunch menu in cultural terms (see the Ethnic/Cultural and Special Audience food guide on the web page listed in the Related Readings). Are religious or cultural needs and differences of students taken into account in preparing the menu? Is there fish on Fridays to accommodate Catholic traditions? Some religious traditions avoid certain foods like pork or all meats. Does your host school accommodate religious traditions like this in any way? In many of the Southern states, for example, pork is used as a common seasoning in many vegetable dishes. What religious dietary requirements are (and are not) accommodated by the school? Are vegetarians accommodated in any way by the school? Think about who participates in the activities in physical education. What strategies could be used to ensure all students would participate in physical education? Judging from the resources and facilities at your school for physical education,

FIG. 5.1.   The Food Guide Pyramid.
http://www.pueblo.gsa.gov/cic_text/food/food-pyramid/main.htm

what importance is placed on healthy bodies in your school?

Related Readings

Black, S. (2000). Nutrition and learning. *American School Board Journal, 187*(2), 49–51.

Ethnic/Cultural and Special Audience Food Guide Pyramid. Retrieved July 20, 2005, from http://www.nal.usda.gov/fnic/etext/000023.html

Hampton, H. (1992). One of the small details that got overlooked: School meals as response to cultural diversity. *Research Papers in Education, 7,* 173–194.

Tynes, S. R. (2001). Bringing social class home: The social class genealogy and poverty lunch projects. *Teaching Sociology, 29,* 286–298.

Cone, S. (2004). Pay me now or pay me later: 10 years and have we seen any change? *Journal of Teaching in Physical Education, 23,* 271–280.

Evans, J., Rich, E., & Davies, B. (2004). The emperor's new clothes: Fat, thin, and overweight. *Journal of Teaching in Physical Education, 23,* 372–391.

Healthy School Food Policies: A Checklist. http://departments.oxy.edu/uepi/ schoolfoodschecklist.htm

NOTES

[1]Berube, M. R. (1994). *American school reform: Progressive, equity and Excellence movements, 1883–1993.* New York: Praeger.

[2]See Spring, J. (2003). *The American school, 1642–2004* (6th ed.). New York: McGraw-Hill.

[3]For an overview of the history of American Education see Spring, J. (2003). *The American school, 1642–2004* (6th ed.). New York: McGraw-Hill. See also, Cremin, L. (1964). *The transformation of the school.* New York: Vantage Books; and Tyack, D. (1974). *The one best system: A history of American urban education.* Cambridge, MA: Harvard University Press.

[4]A nation at risk (April 1993, para. 12). Retrieved December 27, 2004, from http://www.ed.gov/pubs/NatAtRisk/risk.html

[5]A nation at risk (April 1993, para. 12). Retrieved December 27, 2004, from http://www.ed.gov/pubs/NatAtRisk/risk.html

[6]A nation at risk (April 1993, para. 12). Retrieved December 27, 2004, from http://www.ed.gov/pubs/NatAtRisk/risk.html

[7]A nation at risk (April 1993). Retrieved December 27, 2004, from http://www.ed.gov/pubs/NatAtRisk/risk.recomm.html

[8]No Child Left Behind Act of 2001, Pub. L. 107–110, 115 Stat. 1425 (2002).

[9]The ideas for this activity were adapted from personal correspondence with Julie Rucker, doctoral student in curriculum studies at Georgia Southern University.

[10]Cochran-Smith, M. (2005). No Child Left Behind: 3 years and counting. *Journal of Teacher Education, 56,* 99–103.

[11]For more information on the lesser known provision of No Child Left Behind, see C. Chmelynski (2004). NCLB lenient on students' nondisruptive religious practices. *Education Digest, 69,* 36–38; S. Cavanagh (2003). Military recruiters meet pockets of resistance. *Education Week, 22,* 1–2.

[12]Berry, B., Hoke, M., & Hirsch, E. (2004). The search for highly qualified teachers. *Phi Delta Kappan, 85,* 684–689.

[13]Garcia, E. (3rd ed.). (2002). *Student cultural diversity: Understanding and meeting the challenge.* Boston: Houghton Mifflin.

[14]Moll, L. (1992). Funds of knowledge for teaching: Using a qualitative approach to connect homes and classrooms. *Theory Into Practice, 31,* 132–141.

[15]The ideas for this activity were adapted from personal correspondence with Dr. Scott Beck, Assistant Professor, Georgia Southern University.

[16]The ideas for this activity were adapted from personal correspondence with Lee Digiovanni, Assistant Professor of Early Childhood Education, at Georgia College and State University.

[17]See Wellhousen, K., & Martin, N. K. (1995). Preservice teachers and standardized test administration: Their behavioral predictions regarding cheating. *Research in the School, 2,* 47–49.

[18]For more information on race and ethnicity in the 2000 U.S. Census, see Population by race (n.d.). Retrieved July 21, 2005, from http://www.censusscope.org/us/chart_race.html

[19]Thompson, A. (1998). Not for the Color Purple: Black feminist lessons for educational caring. *Harvard Educational Review, 68,* 522–554.

[20]The ideas for this activity were adapted from personal correspondence with Susan Ryan, a doctoral student at Georgia Southern University.

[21]National School Lunch Act citation.

Section 6

After the Field Experience: Now What?

REDESIGNING THE CURRICULUM

Background

Talking about curriculum is like talking about the ocean: The topic is huge, and everybody's perspective is different. Some view curriculum only as the official course of study offered by a school or system of schools. Others see curriculum as including both the official course of study and the hidden, or excluded, knowledge. Although these perspectives are different, they share a common denominator of defining curriculum as content.

There are others who define curriculum in a much broader sense. These individuals understand curriculum as the total package of training that students receive in schools. For these individuals, curriculum exists at multiple levels of openness and awareness. This approach to curriculum also includes what some call "the affective," that is, the transmission of ideology and culturally bound forms of knowledge and action.

There are yet others who define curriculum as existing in all aspects of daily living including the schools. They would argue that television and popular media are powerful curricular models that are very effective forms of teaching under the guise of entertainment, news, information, and so forth. For these individuals, the formal curriculum of schooling is only one small slice of the teaching and learning that occurs every day in our society.

So, where to begin? For the purposes of this section, we construct a double continuum of curriculum. The x-axis represents the range of content to context. That is, on one end, we restrict ourselves to envisioning curriculum as only the formal content of what we teach—the course of study. On the other end is context. According to this view, curriculum encompasses the wide range of social experiences, structures, and forms and is a powerful and always present part of our daily lives in or out of school. The y-axis is the continuum from school to society at large. This considers where curriculum resides. On one extreme, the existence of curriculum is limited only to the school setting. On the other, curriculum is present throughout all social landscapes.

Here, then, in the following diagram, is what we have so far. Remember the x- and y-axes represent continua, not polar opposites.

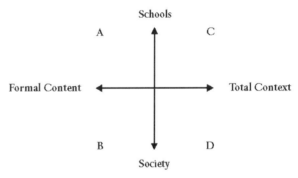

Most of the mainstream work in curriculum reform has taken place in the A and C quadrants. These are the areas that limit the definition of curriculum to the formal content or the course of study for a school or a school system. Frankly, this is also the most easily managed area for thinking about curriculum. Most teachers and education workers place their personal definitions of curriculum within these two quadrants largely because that is how most colleges and universities teach teachers to think about curriculum.

Activity

There have been literally hundreds, if not thousands, of books written in this country in the last century about curriculum and curriculum redesign. We obviously do not try to tackle a subject of such oceanic proportions in one exercise. What we propose is that you go back and review some of your reflective narrative notes and consider additional questions. Hopefully, these questions will position you in such a way as to touch on the breadth of curriculum thought: in other words, all four quadrants.

1. In several exercises, you were asked to consider the nature of your assumptions about other people. How has the content of the formal curriculum helped to shape those assumptions? How might we redesign curricular content to present a more accurate representation of various groups and cultures? Which groups seem to be largely present or missing in the curriculum at large? Think about both the formal curriculum and the manner in which schools are organized (i.e., how schools teach one to act and behave). How might we redesign the way we "do schooling" to be more open and inclusive for all groups?

2. How current or accurate are the textbooks being used in the schools you observed? Are there ways of redesigning the curriculum to make knowledge more appropriate to contemporary and individual needs? Textbooks are largely controlled by publishing houses, state legislatures, and special interest groups. How might the curriculum be redesigned to break this monopoly of power and involve the students and community in the production of knowledge? How might we begin to use and interrogate the larger cultural forms in society (i.e., music, television, films, etc.) as a form of curriculum?

RETHINKING STUDENT–TEACHER RELATIONSHIPS AND LEARNING

Background

We all know that learning is not a one-way activity from teacher to student. Yet, for the most part, we continue to plan lessons in schools as if students were empty vessels waiting to be filled with facts. Most lesson plans, especially at the middle and secondary level, continue to adopt a lecture format, encouraging students to be passive in the education process. Students become proficient at this form of schooling in which they are not held responsible for organizing their own learning.

Such education perpetuates the feeling that what happens in school either has nothing to do with real life or at best is just a preparation for the real world. Thus, students are often "disabled" in their learning instead of becoming empowered and enabled. The curiosity that young children exhibit is stifled in the schools. One major challenge facing educators today is the quest to rekindle this curiosity in order to support the natural curiosity of learners.

How might educators address this problem? Perhaps the relationship between teachers and students can be changed so that learners are encouraged to take a larger role in their own education. How might the fact that teachers are also learners help in alleviating this one-sidedness in schools? How might we redefine learning to encourage a higher level of lifelong learning for everyone in our society? The following activity encourages you to address these concerns.

Activity

Brainstorm about this topic with friends and relatives. Return to your notes and comments that were stimulated by the Reflective Narrative sections of the following activities. Use these notes to guide you in the process of rethinking student–teacher relationships and learning.

1. *Classroom characteristics and climate.* How does the teacher's authoritative style (e.g., autocratic or democratic) affect teacher–student relationships? Which climate did you identify as more effective? Thinking now about how students and teachers relate to one another, do you still find this position more effective? These po-

sitions represent two extremes. What other positions can you articulate as alternatives?

2. *Brain-compatible classrooms.* This activity considers stress generated in classrooms. Review your responses to these questions, and turn your attention to how tension and stress affects teacher–student relationships? Again, at what point does a challenging environment lead to a distant relationship?

3. *Student governance and decision making.* How do student governance issues affect teacher–student relationships? Do governing organizations empower students (all students, some students, which students, and in what ways)? Do some students become disempowered through involvement or exclusion from these organizations? Keep these issues in mind as you rethink these relationships.

Review your responses to the Reflective Narratives from other activities that you have completed. Glean as much information from these reflections as possible to guide you in your exploration of possible student–teacher relationships. Then, record your findings (write a list, make a video or audiotape, etc.). Finally, for each of the discoveries or suggestions you make, generate at least one thing you can do to bring this vision into existence.

REDESIGNING CLASSROOMS

Background

One of the most common assumptions about education is that it must take place in classrooms. Traditionally, we think of classrooms as having four walls, a chalkboard at the front, a teacher's desk in front or back, students' desks arranged in rows, and perhaps a window or two. This exercise challenges you to think beyond this traditional stereotype to generate creative possibilities.

Why must we assume that learning occurs best when students are seated in plastic or wooden desks arranged in straight rows? Is there any reason to believe that staring at the back of another student's head is conducive to learning? Why should students sit at uncomfortable desks instead of on chairs with cushions?

Activity

Recall the questions raised by some of the exercises encountered earlier in this book. On the basis on your own recent observations as well as your prior experiences in school, think about how you might redesign classrooms. Look back at the Reflective Narrative sections of the following exercises for guidance:

1. *Finding a sense of place.* What were the essential features of your special place? How can classroom environments be altered to include these features? What would such a learning environment look like? You might want to make a sketch or drawing of your space.
2. *Metaphors of classroom praxis.* What metaphors did you explore in this exercise? How did these metaphors change the way you think about schools? Use one or more of the metaphors in this exercise to help you think differently about how classrooms are designed.
3. *Sick building/classroom syndrome.* Here you were asked to think about the relation of design to the teaching–learning process. What suggestions did you offer here? How can you implement and include these changes in your classroom design?

Stretch your imagination beyond what you are accustomed to thinking of as a classroom and think about the places, the settings, and the times when you enjoy learning. Brainstorm about how you might redesign classrooms. Explore a variety of labels for classrooms (the metaphors exercise may help here). Think perhaps about outdoor learning centers, educational facilities or nearby corporate buildings, study or quiet areas, and other names that help you expand possibilities for classrooms. Make a list of various possibilities. Make a sketch, paint a picture, or even construct a model of a classroom as you might redesign it.

REDESIGNING TEACHER EDUCATION

Background

In the aftermath of the publication of *A Nation Prepared: Teachers for the 21st Century*,[1] a highly critical report of how colleges and universities were preparing preservice teachers, numerous teacher training programs throughout the United States began making substantial changes in their teacher preparation programs. For example, the Holmes Group, consisting primarily of deans of education at major research universities, promotes the idea of preservice teachers earning a bachelor's degree in liberal arts and a master's degree in education. Similarly, the Project 30 Alliance advocates the addition of more liberal arts courses to teacher preparation. The Renaissance Group, composed primarily of universities that were once teacher-training colleges, asserts that teacher training should begin early in one's university career and that preservice teachers should have extensive experience in the field before student teaching. The National Network for Educational Renewal, founded by John Goodland, believes that reform in public education must go hand in hand with reform in teacher education. Following the footsteps of the National Network for Educational Renewal, many states have adopted P–16 initiatives (i.e., prekindergarten through undergraduate education) that call for co-reform between public education and teacher education programs.

With the passage of the NCLB Act of 2001 in 2002, new demands were made on colleges of education to restructure their teacher education programs to ensure that preservice teachers would meet the highly qualified criteria established by its state. Some colleges of education

have responded by eliminating at the secondary level their undergraduate teacher education program. Other colleges of education have eliminated courses in diversity, social foundations of education, and child development to add additional content-area courses. Critics of NCLB have pointed out that many colleges of education have reacted with a knee-jerk response to these demands and have become little more than "training" schools for future teachers. Others point out that the passage of the NCLB Act with little input from professors of education demonstrates the minimum impact that colleges of education have on policymaking at the state or federal level.

Activities

1. Evaluate your own teacher education program. What courses are mandatory for all education majors? Why do you think these courses are mandatory? How much duplication occurs in your education classes? When do field experiences begin in your program? How much time do you think prospective teachers should spend in classrooms observing, teaching lessons, tutoring students, and so on?

2. Has your teacher preparation program ever been part of any of the preceding reform initiatives? Are they still a part? If not, find out why they no longer participate.

3. Find out what changes your state has made in teacher certification in the last 5 years. What precipitated those changes? What changes were the result of NCLB? Talk to your professors of education and ask them how they have had to respond to NCLB. Do they see these changes as positive or negative?

4. Interview teachers who graduated from your teacher training program within the last 3 years. How well did their university work prepare them for their jobs? What suggestions do they have about reforming teacher education?

5. With a group, brainstorm your response to the following and the implications for teacher

education: Can prospective teachers be taught sensitivity? Can we promote emotional, moral, and spiritual intelligence through teacher education programs? What role can teacher education programs serve in encouraging teachers to develop the self that will inspire our children to become better people?

6. As a group project, recreate your teacher education program in a way that you feel will best prepare preservice teachers to teach schools in the 21st century. Include in your discussion whether the bulk of your courses should be taken in the College of Education or in other colleges on your campus (e.g., College of Liberal Arts). Also, include whether the teacher program should be a 4-year or 5-year program. Share your project with an education professor and/or administrator. What was their reaction to your proposal?

NOTE

[1]Carnegie Forum on Education and the Economy. (1986). *A nation prepared: Teachers for the 21st century*. Washington, DC: The Task Force on Teaching as a Profession. ED 268 120.

Index